Advance praise for Luis Alberto Urrea's
ACROSS THE WIRE

"Luis Alberto Urrea's fine and passionate book about the Mexican poor is nothing less than a travel book to the strange and enduring territory we call the human soul."

—Richard Rodriguez,
author of *Hunger of Memory*

"*Across the Wire* tells of a poverty so immense—it carries over generations, crosses borders, follows lives beyond death, and will haunt your sleep."

—Ana Castillo,
author of *The Mixquiahuala Letters*

"*Across the Wire* graphically portrays life on the trash dumps of Tijuana, a life Luis Alberto Urrea shared with *los de abajo*, those who scratch out a living in the nightmarish world of the *dompes*.

"Those interested in the U.S./Mexico border should read this vivid portrayal of the people who survive in this cesspool which society has created, then forgotten. Urrea has written a work full of despair, yet with flashes of hope, a story which will continue to haunt us. Those forgotten people, Urrea reminds us with compassion, are fellow human beings.

"Urrea deserves recognition for his work among the poor, for reaching out to help the families and the children, and for having the guts to write the story."

—Rudolfo Anaya,
author of *Bless Me, Ultima*

"*Across the Wire* takes you across the cold, objective language and reality described by political discourses into the human tears and laughter that make up daily life at the U.S./Mexico border. I applaud Luis Alberto Urrea for daring to think, speak, and write with emotion . . . for daring to feel in a time of reason."

—Laura Esquivel,
author of *Like Water for Chocolate*

"Like its title, *Across the Wire* is a book that stands at the border between tenderness and anger, death and life. It is an examination of love at the center of devastation, a work of witness, compassion, and finally, of hope."

—Linda Hogan,
author of *Mean Spirit*

"Perhaps only Luis Alberto Urrea could have written this book. Not only because he is a bilingual Chicano, born in Tijuana and raised in San Diego, but also because he is genuinely driven by compassion. Urrea never thinks of the poor as a stereotypic 'they'; he never lets us forget that humor, devotion, and even love can coexist with the most desperate circumstances. A more simplistic writer would anesthetize us to these lives by letting us imagine the poor as dehumanized; Urrea shows us that full humanity persists in situations we would not know how to endure. *Across the Wire* is mostly a book about human suffering, but it never loses hope, and that hope is earned because it is grounded in no illusions. As Urrea says in the end, 'you do what you can'—and he has done what few could do in writing this book."

—Lowry Pei,
author of *Family Resemblances*

"Whether in Egypt, Manila or Tijuana, families who live among garbage—the most abject human living conditions imaginable —are a testament to the spirit of survival. Urrea captures this spirit in his inimitable fashion: straightforward, with plenty of humor, but no gratuitous pity. We learn about life on the U.S./Mexican border, and we learn about ourselves.

"I recommend this book for the general reader, but also for undergraduate students in sociology of poverty, community studies, U.S. and Mexican anthropology and history, and border studies."

—Evelyn Hu-DeHart
Director, Center for Studies of Ethnicity
and Race in America (CSERA),
and Professor of History (Mexico and
Latin America/Caribbean), University
of Colorado at Boulder

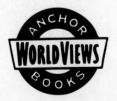

ACROSS THE WIRE

ACROSS THE WIRE

LIFE AND HARD TIMES ON THE MEXICAN BORDER

LUIS ALBERTO URREA

PHOTOGRAPHS BY JOHN LUEDERS-BOOTH

ANCHOR BOOKS
A DIVISION OF RANDOM HOUSE, INC.

NEW YORK

First Anchor Books Edition, January 1993

The stories in this collection are true. Some names
and identities and, especially locations have been changed.
In all cases, accuracy has been
preserved in spite of considerations of security.

Most of the pieces gathered in this volume originally appeared in the San Diego *Reader*, many of them under different titles. They include "Los Cementeros," "Christmas Story," "Father's Day," "Good Friday," "Happy Birthday, Laura Patricia," "The Last Soldier of Pancho Villa," "Meet the Satánicos," "Negra," "Pamplonada," "Tijuana Cop," all the sections of "Sifting Through the Trash," and, finally, portions of the Preface and Prologue.

Library of Congress Cataloging-in-Publication Data
Urrea, Luis Alberto.
Across the wire : life and hard times on the Mexican border / Luis Alberto Urrea : photographs by John Lueders-Booth. — 1st Anchor Books ed.
p. cm.
1. Tijuana (Baja California, Mexico)—Social conditions. 2. Tijuana (Baja California, Mexico)—Economic conditions. 3. Mexican-American Border Region—Social conditions. 4. Mexican-American Border Region—Economic conditions. I. Title.
HN120.T52U77 1993
972′.2—dc20 92-12680
CIP

ISBN 0-385-42530-9

Book design by Bonni Leon
Author photograph on page 191 © 1993 by Barbara Urrea Davis

www.anchorbooks.com

Printed in the United States of America

15 17 19 20 18 16 14

For Von

. . . you were as responsible for everything you saw as you were for everything you did. The problem was that you didn't always know what you were seeing until later, maybe years later, that a lot of it never made it in at all, it just stayed stored there in your eyes.

—Michael Herr,
Dispatches

PREACH WITH YOUR LIFE
NOT WITH YOUR MOUTH

—Hand-painted sign
near the Okefenokee

CONTENTS

Preface   1

Acknowledgments   5

Prologue   9

Chapter One   ·   Sifting Through the Trash   29

Chapter Two   ·   Negra   57

Chapter Three   ·   Los Cementeros   63

Chapter Four   ·   Happy Birthday, Laura Patricia   71

Chapter Five   ·   Good Friday   79

Chapter Six   ·   Pamplonada: A Fire in Tecate   87

Chapter Seven   ·   Tijuana Cop   109

Chapter Eight   ·   The Last Soldier of Pancho Villa   123

Chapter Nine   ·   Meet the Satánicos   133

Chapter Ten   ·   Father's Day   141

Epilogue: Christmas Story   163

PREFACE

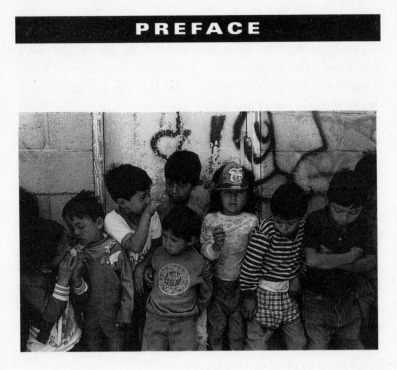

There is a joke told on the border, and it is relished or denounced with equal levels of resignation. It is either a witty take on Cold War rhetoric or a racist epithet politically incorrect in every way. It refers to the hopelessly tattered yet imposing borderline, where thousands of Mexicans pour across every week under helicopters and infrared night-scopes. It refers to the obscure secrets that fester behind the wires, the dastardliness of Mexico that grows into popular myth in our imaginations.

They call the border "the Tortilla Curtain."

This is a book of fragments, stories of moments in the lives of people most of us never see, never think about, and don't even know exist. It seems to me that statements such as "There is a problem on our doorstep" or "The Mexican border is where the third world meets our world" are vague at best. The "huddled masses" ostensibly welcomed by our Statue of Liberty are, specifically, people.

I offer an introduction to the human value in these unknown lives, a story of hope in spite of horror and pain. What you read here happens day and night; the people you meet here live minutes away from you. Learning about their poverty also teaches us about the nature of our wealth.

I do not intend to offer a "balanced" view of our friendly neighbor to the south. Tijuana's boosters always maximize the many wonders of the Borderlands: industry, tourism, bullfights, jai alai, mega-tech discos, duty-free shopping, charming trinkets and baubles, friendly people, even nice beaches on the coast. Any American or well-off Mexican family can see this— all we have to do is drive into town.

Nor is this book a portrait of "the Mexicans." I hope no general inferences are made about the nation or the people. This book is as much an overview of Mexico as a tour of the South Bronx is representative of the entire United States.

Across the Wire deals with my experiences in parts of the Borderlands that no tourist will ever see. It is subjective and biased, and I believe that is the way it should be. I have avoided presenting the people who live there as "noble savages." Poverty ennobles no one; it brutalizes common people and makes them hungry and old.

Most of the people in these pieces urged me to tell their

stories. They believed that if you knew where and how they lived, then they wouldn't simply fade away, relegated to as pointless a death as the lives they had been forced to live.

Although there are missionaries here, and their roles often make them heroic in the context of this book, it is not my intent to offer religious homilies. There will be no altar call at the end of the book. However, it has become obvious to me that the role of missionaries is a subject of serious question on many counts. I cannot speak for any other missionary group's agenda or actions; this is not intended as a sweeping overview of spiritual service or anthropological damage. Rather, I focus on the activities of one basically decent and slightly renegade group.

Most of this manuscript was wrung from about fifteen hundred pages of notes gathered on my travels with the missionaries from 1978 to 1982. Several times during 1982–85 I returned to the Borderlands from an East Coast teaching position. Finally, I researched the region anew as a writer for the San Diego *Reader* in the summer and winter of 1990. The *Reader* gave me the opportunity to disseminate these dark secrets to hundreds of thousands of people in California. Always surprising to me was that San Diegans, living right beside the border, had no idea what went on there. If they didn't know, the rest of the world knew even less.

More startling was that Mexicans didn't know, or pretended not to know. My Mexican family didn't know. This, in spite of having always lived in Tijuana, of seeing the shacks in the hills, of deflecting the beggars, the shoeshine boys, and the gum-selling girls.

I have come to believe that when something is this bad, we

look the other way, or we hope it's better than it looks. I trust this book will put a face on the "huddled masses" who are invading our borders. I want you to know why they're coming.

Luis Alberto Urrea
Boulder, Colorado
1992

ACKNOWLEDGMENTS

This book grew over a long period of time—from 1979 to 1992. Clearly, I did not create it alone. Many hands tended to it —and to me—over these long years. I owe thanks to those both named and unnamed, and I hope the latter will forgive any lapses on my part.

I must begin by offering my deepest gratitude and respect to the people of Tijuana and the border region; their honesty, goodwill, and faith stay with me always. In particular, I owe a debt to Ana María Cervantes Calderón—La Negra—who has taught me much about courage.

There can't be enough thanks for my wife, Barbara Urrea Davis, for her fearlessness as a border rat and an editor, and for her companionship and support.

To Pastor Von: I owe this book to you, Von. Thank you for more than I can express here. I also must thank the good people of Spectrum Ministries, Inc., San Diego, California. All the workers and missionaries and adventurers who came and went over the long haul are far too many to name here. A blanket "thank you" will have to suffice. However, two co-conspirators, Victor Harris and Steven Van Belle, must be mentioned. Also, of the Mexico Crew, thanks especially to Judy Frye, Cindy Harris, Steven Mierau, Judi Mills, Clara Norris, Mike Sliffe, Sharleen Turner, Kyle Wiggins. And a special greeting to Efren, Mary-Alice, and Javier.

Thanks to agent provocateur Thomas Hart for unflagging faith. To my editor, Deborah Ackerman.

To 91X (XETRA-FM, San Diego). And to the Worst Deejay on Earth: the Mighty Oz. Thanks and love to Cynthia Jeffery. And thanks to the Trash Can Sinatras; Country Dick Montana of the Beat Farmers; and Chas, formerly of Madness. Also, deepest thanks to Jim Holman and the San Diego *Reader*. Thanks, also, to the glorious Jeanette King; and to Sue Greenberg, Linda Nevin, Leslie Venolia, Jeanette De Wyze.

To César A. González-T., mentor and teacher; and to Michael R. Ornelas, good friend and homey. While I wrote the first batch of these notes, I was employed by San Diego Mesa College Chicano Studies Department, and Mike and César allowed me every Thursday, most Tuesdays, most Fridays, and far too many Mondays away from work.

To the cast members of the UCSD Hispanic Theater Program/Teatro Máscara Mágica, who bravely entered the dumps and *barrios*, then offered these stories back to the public: Peter Cirino, Sol Miranda, Armando Ortega, Raúl Ramos, Carmen Elena Sosa, Michael Torres, Luis "Wilo" Tristani, Wanda Vega. Laura Esparza and Roberto Gutiérrez. And thanks to director José Luis Valenzuela and producer Jorge Huerta—for insight and vision. Finally, to Nancy Griffiths, who started the ball.

To my late mother, Phyllis, who worked ceaselessly for the Mexican poor. At Harvard: to brother Jack Booth, photographic genius. At U. of Colorado, Boulder: to Lorna Dee Cervantes, Jay Griswold, Salvador Rodríguez del Pino, Linda Hogan, Marilyn Krysl, Evelyn Hu-DeHart, Peter Michelson, Rick Williams. And, *especially*, to the indispensable Janet Hard.

A final riot of thanks—"propers" due to so many who lent a hand. To Patricia Ammann, Rudy Anaya, Judy Bell, Duane Brewer. To Becca Carmona, Diana Casebolt (née Whitney). To the Davis family—especially Peg for her proofreading assistance. And to Bertha Edington and Rick Elias: thanks a lot.

To Chancellor Auggie Gallego of the San Diego Community College District.

To John Garwood, Jock Gaynor: the movie men. Thank you, Bette González. To Cindy Hanes, Margaret Hart. To Ursula K. Le Guin, with lurve. To Mike Lowery, Richard Marius, Michele Moore, Haas Mrue, Simone Muench. To Lyn Niles, for everything. To Mad Dog Lowry Pei. To Darcy Peters, Jeff Schafer. For sanity, thanks always to Kenneth L. Sipe of Wellesley, MA. Special thanks to Suzy Tanzer for her kind generosity and friendship. And to Lily Tomlin—you brought me back to life.

To los Urrea—Juan, Luis Octavio, Lety, Alberto, y Martha; Hugo Millan; and *un abrazo fuerte para* Sra. Emilia Zazueta de Urrea.

To my good friend Jon Urshan. To Caty Van Housen.

And to Shawn Phillips and his late father, Philip Atlee (James Atlee Phillips)—thank you.

Finally, to David Thomson—when others fell away, you were the last man standing.

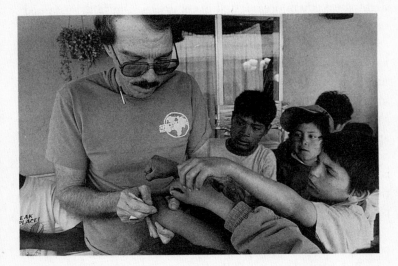

Border Story

When I was younger, I went to war. The Mexican border was the battlefield. There are many Mexicos; there are also many Mexican borders, any one of which could fill its own book. I, and the people with me, fought on a specific front. We sustained injuries and witnessed deaths. There were machine guns pointed at us, knives, pistols, clubs, even skyrockets. I caught a street-gang member trying to stuff a lit cherry bomb into our gas tank. On the same night, a drunk mariachi opened fire on the missionaries through the wall of his house.

We drove five beat-up vans. We were armed with water, medicine, shampoo, food, clothes, milk, and doughnuts. At the end of a day, like returning veterans from other battles, we carried secrets in our hearts that kept some of us awake at night, gave others dreams and fits of crying. Our faith sustained us—if not in God or "good," then in our work.

Others of us had no room for or interest in such drama, and came away unscathed—and unmoved. Some of us sank into the mindless joy of fundamentalism, some of us drank, some of us married impoverished Mexicans. Most of us took it personally. Poverty *is* personal: it smells and it shocks and it invades your space. You come home dirty when you get too close to the poor. Sometimes you bring back vermin: they hide in your hair, in your underpants, in your intestines. These unpleasant possibilities are a given. They are the price you occasionally have to pay.

In Tijuana and environs, we met the many ambassadors of poverty: lice, scabies, tapeworm, pinworm, ringworm, fleas, crab lice. We met diphtheria, meningitis, typhoid, polio, *turista* (diarrhea), tuberculosis, hepatitis, VD, impetigo, measles, chronic hernia, malaria, whooping cough. We met madness and "demon possession."

These were the products of dirt and disregard—bad things afflicting good people. Their world was far from our world. Still, it would take you only about twenty minutes to get there from the center of San Diego.

For me, the worst part was the lack of a specific enemy. We were fighting a nebulous, all-pervasive *It*. Call it hunger. Call it despair. Call it the Devil, the System, Capitalism, the Cycle of

Poverty, the Fruits of the Mexican Malaise. It was a seemingly endless circle of disasters. Long after I'd left, the wheel kept on grinding.

At night, the Border Patrol helicopters swoop and churn in the air all along the line. You can sit in the Mexican hills and watch them herd humans on the dusty slopes across the valley. They look like science fiction crafts, their hard-focused lights raking the ground as they fly.

Borderlands locals are so jaded by the sight of nightly people-hunting that it doesn't even register in their minds. But take a stranger to the border, and she will *see* the spectacle: monstrous Dodge trucks speeding into and out of the landscape; uniformed men patrolling with flashlights, guns, and dogs; spotlights; running figures; lines of people hurried onto buses by armed guards; and the endless clatter of the helicopters with their harsh white beams. A Dutch woman once told me it seemed altogether "un-American."

But the Mexicans keep on coming—and the Guatemalans, the Salvadorans, the Panamanians, the Colombians. The seven-mile stretch of Interstate 5 nearest the Mexican border is, at times, so congested with Latin American pedestrians that it resembles a town square.

They stick to the center island. Running down the length of the island is a cement wall. If the "illegals" (currently, "undocumented workers"; formerly, "wetbacks") are walking north and a Border Patrol vehicle happens along, they simply hop over the wall and trot south. The officer will have to drive up to the 805 interchange, or Dairy Mart Road, swing over the overpasses, then drive south. Depending on where this pursuit begins, his detour could entail five to ten miles of driving. When the officer finally reaches the group, they hop over the wall and trot north. Furthermore, because freeway arrests would endanger traffic, the Border Patrol has effectively thrown up its hands in surrender.

It seems jolly on the page. But imagine poverty, violence, natural disasters, or political fear driving you away from everything you know. Imagine how bad things get to make you leave behind your family, your friends, your lovers; your home, as humble as it might be; your church, say. Let's take it further—you've said good-bye to the graveyard, the dog, the goat, the mountains where you first hunted, your grade school, your state, your favorite spot on the river where you fished and took time to think.

Then you come hundreds—or thousands—of miles across territory utterly unknown to you. (Chances are, you have never traveled farther than a hundred miles in your life.) You have walked, run, hidden in the backs of trucks, spent part of your precious money on bus fare. There is no AAA or Travelers Aid Society available to you. Various features of your journey north might include police corruption; violence in the forms of beatings, rape, murder, torture, road accidents; theft; incarceration. Additionally, you might experience loneliness, fear, exhaustion, sorrow, cold, heat, diarrhea, thirst, hunger. There is no medical attention available to you. There isn't even Kotex.

Weeks or months later, you arrive in Tijuana. Along with other immigrants, you gravitate to the bad parts of town because there is nowhere for you to go in the glittery sections where the *gringos* flock. You stay in a run-down little hotel in the red-light district, or behind the bus terminal. Or you find your way to the garbage dumps, where you throw together a small cardboard nest and claim a few feet of dirt for yourself. The garbage-pickers working this dump might allow you to squat, or they might come and rob you or burn you out for breaking some local rule you cannot possibly know beforehand. Sometimes the dump is controlled by a syndicate, and goon squads might come to you within a day. They want money, and if you can't pay, you must leave or suffer the consequences.

In town, you face endless victimization if you aren't streetwise. The police come after you, street thugs come after you, petty criminals come after you; strangers try your door at night as you sleep. Many shady men offer to guide you across the border, and each one wants all your money now, and promises to meet you at a prearranged spot. Some of your fellow travelers end their journeys right here—relieved of their savings and left to wait on a dark corner until they realize they are going nowhere.

If you are not Mexican, and can't pass as *tijuanense*, a local, the tough guys find you out. Salvadorans and Guatemalans are routinely beaten up and robbed. Sometimes they are disfigured. Indians—Chinantecas, Mixtecas, Guasaves, Zapotecas, Mayas—are insulted and pushed around; often they are lucky—they are merely ignored. They use this to their advantage. Often they don't dream of crossing into the United States: a Mexican tribal person would never be able to blend in, and they know it. To them, the garbage dumps and street vending and begging in Tijuana are a vast improvement over their former lives. As Doña Paula, a Chinanteca friend of mine who lives at the Tijuana garbage dump, told me, "This is the garbage dump. Take all you need. There's plenty here for *everyone!*"

If you are a woman, the men come after you. You lock yourself in your room, and when you must leave it to use the pestilential public bathroom at the end of your floor, you hurry, and you check every corner. Sometimes the lights are out in the toilet room. Sometimes men listen at the door. They call you "good-looking" and "bitch" and "*mamacita,*" and they make kissing sounds at you when you pass.

You're in the worst part of town, but you can comfort yourself—at least there are no death squads here. There are no torturers here, or bandit land barons riding into your house. This is the last barrier, you think, between you and the United States—*los Yunaites Estaites.*

You still face police corruption, violence, jail. You now also have a wide variety of new options available to you: drugs, prostitution, white slavery, crime. Tijuana is not easy on new-comers. It is a city that has always thrived on taking advantage of a sucker. And the innocent are the ultimate suckers in the Borderlands.

If you have saved up enough money, you go to one of the *coyotes* (people-smugglers), who guide travelers through the violent canyons immediately north of the border. Lately, these men are also called *polleros,* or "chicken-wranglers." Some of them are straight, some are land pirates. Negotiations are tense and strange: *polleros* speak a Spanish you don't quite understand— like the word *polleros.* Linguists call the new border-speak "Spanglish," but in Tijuana, Spanglish is mixed with slang and *pochismos* (the polyglot hip talk of Mexicans infected with *gringoismo;* the *cholos* in Mexico, or Chicanos on the American side).

Suddenly, the word for "yes," *sí,* can be *simón* or *siról.* "No" is *chale.* "Bike" *(bicicleta)* is *baica.* "Wife" *(esposa)* is *waifa.* "The police" *(la policía)* are *la chota.* "Women" are *rucas* or *morras.* You don't know what they're talking about.

You pay them all your money—sometimes it's your family's lifelong savings. Five hundred dollars should do it. *"Orale,"* the dude tells you, which means "right on." You must wait in Colonia Libertad, the most notorious *barrio* in town, ironically named "Liberty."

The scene here is baffling. Music blares from radios. Jolly women at smoky taco stands cook food for the journeys, sell jugs of water. You can see the Border Patrol agents cruising the other side of the fence; they trade insults with the locals.

When the appointed hour comes, you join a group of *pollos* (chickens) who scuttle along behind the *coyote*. You crawl under the wires, or, if you go a mile east, you might be amazed to find that the famous American Border Fence simply stops. To enter the United States, you merely step around the end of it. And you follow your guide into the canyons. You might be startled to find groups of individuals crossing the line without *coyotes* leading them at all. You might wonder how they have mastered the canyons, and you might begin to regret the loss of your money.

If you have your daughters or mothers or wives with you—or if you are a woman—you become watchful and tense, because rape and gang rape are so common in this darkness as to be utterly unremarkable. If you have any valuables left after your various negotiations, you try to find a sly place to hide them in case you meet *pandilleros* (gang members) or *rateros* (thieves—ratmen). But, really, where can you put anything? Thousands have come before you, and the hiding places are pathetically obvious to robbers: in shoulder bags or clothing rolls, pinned inside clothes, hidden in underwear, inserted in body orifices.

If the *coyote* does not turn on you suddenly with a gun and take everything from you himself, you might still be attacked by the *rateros*. If the *rateros* don't get you, there are roving zombies that you can smell from fifty yards downwind—these are the junkies who hunt in shambling packs. If the junkies somehow miss you, there are the *pandilleros*—gang-bangers from either side of the border who are looking for some bloody fun. They adore "taking off" illegals because it's the perfect crime: there is no way they can ever be caught. They are Tijuana *cholos*, or Chicano *vatos*, or Anglo head-bangers.

Their sense of fun relies heavily on violence. Gang beatings are their preferred sport, though rape in all its forms is common, as always. Often the *coyote* will turn tail and run at the first sight of *pandilleros*. What's another load of desperate chickens to him? He's just making a living, taking care of business.

If he doesn't run, there is a good chance he will be the first to be assaulted. The most basic punishment these young toughs mete out is a good beating, but they might kill him in front of the *pollos* if they feel the immigrants need a lesson in obedience. For good measure, these boys—they are mostly *boys*, aged twelve to nineteen, bored with Super Nintendo and MTV—beat people and slash people and thrash the women they have just finished raping.

Their most memorable tactic is to hamstring the *coyote* or anyone who dares speak out against them. This entails slicing the muscles in the victim's legs and leaving him to flop around in the dirt, crippled. If you are in a group of *pollos* that happens to be visited by these furies, you are learning border etiquette.

Now, say you are lucky enough to evade all these dangers on your journey. Hazards still await you and your family. You might meet white racists, complimenting themselves with the tag "Aryans"; they "patrol" the scrub in combat gear, carrying radios, high-powered flashlights, rifles, and bats. Rattlesnakes hide in bushes—you didn't count on that complication. Scorpions, tarantulas, black widows. And, of course, there is the Border Patrol *(la migra)*.

They come over the hills on motorcycles, on horses, in huge Dodge Ramcharger four-wheel drives. They yell, wear frightening goggles, have guns. Sometimes they are surprisingly decent; sometimes they are too tired or too bored to put much effort into dealing with you. They collect you in a large group of fellow *pollos,* and a guard (a Mexican Border Patrol agent!) jokes with your group in Spanish. Some cry, some sulk, most laugh. Mexicans hate to be rude. You don't know what to think—some of your fellow travelers take their arrest with aplomb. Sometimes the officers know their names. But you have been told repeatedly that the Border Patrol sometimes beats or kills people. Everyone talks about the Mexican girl molested inside its building.

The Border Patrol puts you into trucks that take you to buses that take you to compounds that load you onto other buses that transport you back to Tijuana and put you out. Your *coyote* isn't bothered in the least. Some of the regulars who were with you go across and get brought back a couple of times a night. But for you, things are different. You have been brought back with no place to sleep. You have already spent all your money. You might have been robbed, so you have only your clothes—maybe not all of them. The robbers may have taken your shoes. You might be bloodied from a beating by *pandilleros,* or an "accident" in the Immigration and Naturalization Service compound. You can't get proper medical attention. You can't eat, or afford to feed your family. Some of your compatriots have been separated from their wives or their children. Now their loved ones are in the hands of strangers, in the vast and unknown United States. The Salvadorans are put on planes and flown back to the waiting arms of the military. As you walk through the cyclone fence, back into Tijuana, the locals taunt you and laugh at your misfortune.

If you were killed, you have nothing to worry about.

Now what?

Perhaps you'll join one of the other groups that break through the Tortilla Curtain every night. The road-runners. They amass at dusk along the cement canal that separates the United States from Mexico. This wide alley is supposedly the Tijuana River, but it's usually dry, or running with sewage that Tijuana pumps toward the U.S. with great gusto.

As soon as everybody feels like it—there are no *coyotes* needed here—you join the groups passing through the gaping holes in the fence. Houses and alleys and cantinas back up against it, and in some spots, people have driven stolen cars into the poles to provide a wider passage. You rush across the canal and up the opposite slope, timing your dash between passing *migra* trucks and the overflights of helicopters. Following the others, you begin your jog toward the freeway. Here, there are mostly just Border Patrol officers to outrun—not that hard if you're in good shape. There are still some white-supremacist types bobbling around, but the cops will get them if they do anything serious. No, here the problem is the many lanes of I-5.

You stand at the edge of the road and wonder how you're going to cut across five lanes of traffic going sixty miles an hour. Then, there is the problem of the next five lanes. The freeway itself is constructed to run parallel to the border, then swing north. Its underpasses and storm-drain pipes offer another sub-

terranean world, but you don't know about them. All you know
is you have to get across at some point, and get far from the
hunters who would take you back.

If you hang around the shoulder of I-5 long enough, you will
find that many of your companions don't make it. So many have
been killed and injured that the *gringos* have put up warning
signs to motorists to watch for running people. The orange signs
show a man, a woman, and a child charging across. Some *gringos* are so crazy with hate for you that they speed up, or aim for
you as you run.

The vague blood of over a hundred slain runners shadows
the concrete.

On either side of the border, clustered near the gates, there
are dapper-looking men, dressed in nice cowboy clothes, and
they speak without looking anyone in the eye. They are saying,
"Los Angeles. San Bernardino. San Francisco."

They have a going concern: business is good.

Once you've gotten across the line, there will always be the
question of *Where do I go now?* "Illegal aliens" have to eat,
sleep, find work. Once across, you must begin another journey.

Not everyone has the energy to go on. Even faith—in Jesus,
the Virgin Mary, or the Streets of Gold—breaks down sooner or
later. Many of these immigrants founder at the border. There is
a sad swirl of humanity in Tijuana. Outsiders eddy there who
have simply run out of strength. If North America does not want
them, Tijuana wants them even less. They become the outcasts
of an outcast region. We could all see them if we looked hard
enough: they sell chewing gum. Their children sing in traffic. In

bars downtown, the women will show us a breast for a quarter. They wash our windshields at every stoplight. But mostly, they are invisible. To see them, we have to climb up the little canyons all around the city, where the cardboard shacks and mud and smoke look like a lost triptych by Hieronymus Bosch. We have to wade into the garbage dumps and the orphanages, sit in the little churches and the hospitals, or go out into the back country, where they raise their goats and bake red bricks and try to live decent lives.

They are not welcome in Tijuana. And, for the most part, Tijuana itself is not welcome in the Motherland. Tijuana is Mexico's cast-off child. She brings in money and *gringos,* but nobody would dare claim her. As a Mexican diplomat once confided to me, "We both know Tijuana is not Mexico. The border is nowhere. It's a no-man's-land."

I was born there.

My Story

I was born in Tijuana, to a Mexican father and an American mother. I was registered with the U.S. government as an American Citizen, Born Abroad. Raised in San Diego, I crossed the border all through my boyhood with abandon, utterly bilingual and bicultural. In 1977, my father died on the border, violently. (The story is told in detail in a chapter entitled "Father's Day.")

In the Borderlands, anything can happen. And if you're in Tijuana long enough, anything *will* happen. Whole neighborhoods appear and disappear seemingly overnight. For example, when I was a boy, you got into Tijuana by driving through the Tijuana River itself. It was a muddy floodplain bustling with animals and belching old cars. A slum that spread across the riverbed was known as "Cartolandia." In border-speak, this meant "Land of Cardboard."

Suddenly, it was time for Tijuana to spruce up its image to attract more American dollars, and Cartolandia was swept away by a flash flood of tractors. The big machines swept down the length of the river, crushing shacks and toppling fences. It was like magic. One week, there were choked multitudes of sheds; the next, a clear, flat space awaiting the blank concrete of a flood channel. Town—no town.

The inhabitants of Cartolandia fled to the outskirts, where they were better suited to Tijuana's new image as Shopping Mecca. They had effectively vanished. Many of them homesteaded the Tijuana municipal garbage dump. The city's varied orphanages consumed many of their children.

Tijuana's characteristic buzz can be traced directly to a mixture of dread and expectation: there's always something coming.

I never intended to be a missionary. I didn't go to church, and I had no reason to believe I'd be involved with a bunch of Baptists. But in 1978, I had occasion to meet a remarkable preacher known as Pastor Von (Erhardt George von Trutzschler III, no less): as well as being a minister, he was a veteran of the Korean War, a graphic artist, a puppeteer, a German baron, an adventurer, and a practical joker. Von got me involved in the hardships and discipline he calls "Christian Boot Camp."

After working as a youth pastor in San Diego for many years, he had discovered Mexico in the late sixties. His work there began with the typical church do-good activities that everyone has experienced at least once: a bag of blankets for the orphans, a few Christmas toys, alms for the poor. As Protestantism spread in Mexico, however, interest in Von's preaching grew. Small churches and Protestant orphanages and Protestant *barrios,* lacking ministers of their own, began asking Von to teach. Preaching and pastoring led to more work; work led to more needs; more needs pulled in more workers. On it went until Von had put in thirty or so years slogging through the Borderlands mud, and his little team of die-hard renegades and border rats had grown to a nonprofit corporation (Spectrum Ministries, Inc.), where you'll find him today.

Von's religious ethic is similar in scope to Teresa of Calcutta's. Von favors actual works over heavy evangelism. Spectrum is based on a belief Christians call "living the gospel." This doctrine is increasingly rare in America, since it involves little lip service, hard work, and no glory.

Von often reminds his workers that they are "ambassadors of Christ" and should comport themselves accordingly. Visitors are indelicately stripped of their misconceptions and prejudices when they discover that the crust on Von and his crew is a mile thick: the sight of teenybopper Bible School girls enduring Von's lurid pretrip briefing is priceless. Insouciantly, he offers up his litany: lice, worms, pus, blood; diarrhea, rattletrap outhouses, no toilet paper; dangerous water and food; diseased animals that will leave you with scabies; rats, maggots, flies; *odor.* Then he confuses them by demanding love and respect for the poor. He caps his talk with: "Remember—you are not going to the zoo. These are people. Don't run around snapping pictures of them like they're animals. Don't rush into their shacks saying, 'Ooh, gross!' They live there. Those are their homes."

Because border guards often "confiscate" chocolate milk, the cartons must be smuggled into Mexico under bags of clothes. Because the floors of the vans get so hot, the milk will curdle, so the crew must first freeze it. The endless variations of challenge in the Borderlands keep Von constantly alert—problems come three at a time and must be solved on the run.

Like the time a shipment of tennis shoes was donated to Spectrum. They were new, white, handsome shoes. The only problem was that no two shoes in the entire shipment matched. Von knew there was no way the Mexican kids could use *one* shoe, and they—like teens everywhere—were fashion-conscious and wouldn't be caught dead in unmatching sneakers.

Von's solution was practical and witty. He donned unmatched shoes and made his crew members wear unmatched shoes. Then he announced that it was the latest California surfer rage; kids in California weren't considered hip unless they wore unmatched shoes. The shipment was distributed, and shoeless boys were shod in the *faux* fashion craze begun by Chez Von.

Von has suffered for his beliefs. In the ever more conservative atmosphere of American Christianity (read: Protestantism), the efforts of Spectrum have come under fire on several occasions. He was once denounced because he refused to use the King James Bible in his sermons—clearly the sign of a heretic.

Von's terse reply to criticism: "It's hard to 'save' people when they're dead."

Von has a Monday night ministerial run into Tijuana, and in his heyday, he was hitting three or four orphanages a night. I was curious, unaware of the severity of the poverty in Tijuana. I knew it was there, but it didn't really mean anything to me. One night, in late October 1978, my curiosity got the better of me. I didn't believe Von could show me anything about my hometown that I didn't know. I was wrong. I quickly began to learn just how little I really knew.

He managed to get me involved on the first night. Actually, it was Von and a little girl named América. América lived in one of the orphanages barely five miles from my grandmother's house in the hills above Tijuana.

She had light hair and blue eyes like mine—she could have been my cousin. When she realized I spoke Spanish, she clutched my fingers and chattered for an hour without a break. She hung on harder when Von announced it was time to go. She begged me not to leave. América resorted to a tactic many orphanage children master to keep visitors from leaving—she wrapped her legs around my calf and sat on my foot. As I peeled her off, I promised to return on Von's next trip.

He was waiting for me in the alley behind the orphanage.

"What did you say to that girl?" he asked.

"I told her I'd come back next week."

He glared at me. "Don't *ever* tell one of my kids you're coming back," he snapped. "Don't you know she'll wait all week for you? Then she'll wait for months. Don't say it if you don't mean it."

"I mean it!" I said.

I went back the next time to see her. Then again. And, of course, there were other places to go before we got to América's orphanage, and there were other people to talk to after we left. Each location had people waiting with messages and questions to translate. It didn't take long for Von to approach me with a proposition. It seemed he had managed the impressive feat of spending a lifetime in Mexico without picking up any Spanish at all. Within two months, I was Von's personal translator.

It is important to note that translation is often more delicate an art than people assume. For example, Mexicans are regularly amused to read *TV Guide* listings for Spanish-language TV stations. If one were to leave the tilde (˜) off the word *años*, or "years," the word becomes the plural for "anus." Many cheap laughs are had when "The Lost Years" becomes "The Lost Butt Holes."

It was clear that Von needed reliable translating. Once, when he had arranged a summer camping trip for *barrio* children, he'd written a list of items the children needed to take. A well-meaning woman on the team translated the list for Von, and they Xeroxed fifty or sixty copies.

The word for "comb" in Spanish is *peine*, but leave out a letter, and the word takes on a whole new meaning. Von's note, distributed to every child and all their families, read:

You must bring CLEAN CLOTHES
TOOTH PASTE
SOAP
TOOTHBRUSH
SLEEPING BAG
and BOYS—You Must Remember
to BRING YOUR PENIS!

Von estimates that in a ten-year period his crew drove several *million* miles in Mexico without serious incident. Over five hundred people came and went as crew members. They transported more than sixty thousand visitors across the border.

In my time with him, I saw floods and three hundred-mile-wide prairie fires, car wrecks and gang fights, monkeys and blood and shit. I saw human intestines and burned flesh. I saw human fat through deep red cuts. I saw people copulating. I saw animals tortured. I saw birthday parties in the saddest sagging shacks. I looked down throats and up wombs with flashlights. I saw lice, rats, dying dogs, rivers black with pollywogs, and a mound of maggots three feet wide and two feet high. One little boy in the back country cooked himself with an overturned pot of boiling *frijoles;* when I asked him if it hurt, he sneered like Pancho Villa and said, "Nah." A maddened Pentecostal tried to heal our broken-down van by laying hands on the engine block. One girl who lived in a brickyard accidentally soaked her dress in diesel fuel and lit herself on fire. When I went in the shed, she was standing there, naked, her entire front burned dark brown and red. The only part of her not burned was her vulva; it was a startling cleft, a triangular island of white in a sea of burns.

I saw miracles, too. A boy named Chispi, deep in a coma induced by spinal meningitis, suffered a complete shutdown of one lobe of his brain. The doctors in the intensive care unit, looking down at his naked little body hard-wired to banks of machinery and pumps, just shook their heads. He was doomed to be a vegetable, at best. His mother, fished out of the cantinas in Tijuana's red-light district, spent several nights sitting in the hospital cafeteria sipping vending-machine coffee and telling me she hoped there were miracles left for people like her.

Chispi woke up. The machines were blipping and pinging, and he sat up and asked for Von. His brain had regenerated itself. They unhitched him, pulled out the catheters, and pulled the steel shunt out of his skull. He went home. There was no way anybody could explain it. Sometimes there were happy endings, and you spent as much time wondering about them as grieving over the tragedies.

God help me—it was fun. It was exciting and nasty. I strode, fearless, through the Tijuana garbage dumps and the Barrio of Shallow Graves. I was doing good deeds, and the goodness thrilled me. But the squalor, too, thrilled me. Each stinking gray *barrio* gave me a wicked charge. I was arrested one night by Tijuana cops; I was so terrified that my knees wobbled like Jell-O. After they let me go, I was happy for a week. Mexican soldiers pointed machine guns at my testicles. I thought I was going to die. Later, I was so relieved, I laughed about it for days. Over the years, I was cut, punctured, sliced: I love my scars. I had girlfriends in every village, in every orphanage, at each garbage dump. For a time, I was a hero. And at night, when we returned, caked in dried mud, smelly, exhausted, and the good Baptists of Von's church looked askance at us, we felt dangerous. The housewives, grandmothers, fundamentalists, rock singers, bikers, former drug dealers, schoolgirls, leftists, republicans, jarheads, and I were all transformed into *The Wild Bunch.*

It added a certain flair to my dating life as well. It was not uncommon for a Mexican crisis to track me down in the most unlikely places. I am reminded of the night I was sitting down to a fancy supper at a woman's apartment when the phone rang. A busload of kids from one of our orphanages had flipped over, killing the American daughter of the youth minister in charge of the trip. All the *gringos* had been arrested. The next hour was spent calling Tijuana cops, Mexican lawyers, cousins in Tijuana, and Von. I had to leave early to get across the border.

Incredibly, in the wake of this tragedy, the orphanage kids were taken to the beach by yet another *gringo* church group, and one of the boys was hit by a car and killed.

My date was fascinated by all this, no doubt.

Slowly, it became obvious that nobody outside the experience understood it. Only among ourselves was hunting for lice in each other's hair considered a nice thing. Nobody but us found humor in the appalling things we saw. No one else wanted to discuss the particulars of our bowel movements. By firsthand experience, we had become diagnosticians in the area of gastrointestinal affliction. Color and content spoke volumes to us: pale, mucus-heavy ropes of diarrhea suggested amoebas. Etc.

One of Von's pep talks revolved around the unconscionable wealth in the United States. "Well," he'd say to some unsuspecting *gringo*, "you're probably not rich. You probably don't even have a television. Oh, you *do?* You have three televisions? One in each room? Wow. But surely you don't have furniture? You do? Living room furniture and beds in the bedrooms? Imagine that!

"But you don't have a floor, do you? Do you have carpets? Four walls? A roof! What do you use for light—candles? *Lamps!* No way. Lamps.

"How about your kitchen—do you have a stove?"

He'd pick his way through the kitchen: the food, the plates and pots and pans, the refrigerator, the ice. Ice cream. Soda. Booze. The closets, the clothes in the closets. Then to the bathroom and the miracle of indoor plumbing. Whoever lived in that house suddenly felt obscenely rich.

I was never able to reach Von's level of commitment. The time he caught scabies, he allowed it to flourish in order to grasp the suffering of those from whom it originated. He slept on the floor because the majority of the world's population could not afford a bed.

CHAPTER ONE

SIFTING THROUGH THE TRASH

Trash

One of the most beautiful views of San Diego is from the summit of a small hill in Tijuana's municipal garbage dump. People live on that hill, picking through the trash with long poles that end in hooks made of bent nails. They scavenge for bottles, tin, aluminum, cloth; for cast-out beds, wood, furniture. Sometimes they find meat that is not too rotten to be cooked.

This view-spot is where the city drops off its dead animals —dogs, cats, sometimes goats, horses. They are piled in heaps six feet high and torched. In that stinking blue haze, amid nightmarish sculptures of charred ribs and carbonized tails, the garbage-pickers can watch the buildings of San Diego gleam gold on the blue coastline. The city looks cool in the summer when heat cracks the ground and flies drill into their noses. And in the winter, when windchill drops night temperatures into the low thirties, when the cold makes their lips bleed, and rain turns the hill into a gray pudding of ash and mud, and babies are wrapped in plastic trash bags for warmth, San Diego glows like a big electric dream. And every night on that burnt hill, these people watch.

In or near every Mexican border town, you will find trash dumps. Some of the bigger cities have more than one "official" dump, and there are countless smaller, unlicensed places piled with garbage. Some of the official dumps are quite large, and some, like the one outside Tecate, are small and well hidden. People live in almost every one of them.

Each *dompe* has its own culture, as distinct as the people living there. (*Dompe* is border-speak, a word in neither Spanish nor English. It is an attempt to put a North American word or concept—"dump"—into a Mexican context. Thus, "junkyard" becomes *yonke* and "muffler" becomes *mofle*.) Each of these *dompes* has its own pecking order. Certain people are "in." Some families become power brokers due to their relationships to the missionaries who invariably show up, bearing bags of old clothes and vanloads of food. Some *dompes* even have "mayors"; some have hired goons, paid off by shady syndicates, to keep the trash-pickers in line. It's a kind of illegal serfdom, where the poor must pay a ransom to the rich to pick trash to survive.

Then there are those who are so far "out" that the mind reels. In the Tijuana *dompe*, the outcasts were located along the western edge of the settlement in shacks and lean-tos, in an area known as "the pig village." This was where the untouchables of this society of untouchables slept, among the pigs awaiting slaughter.

I knew them all: the Serranos, the Cheese Lady, Pacha, Jesusita.

A Woman Called Little Jesus

It was raining. It had been raining for weeks, and the weather was unremittingly cold. The early-morning van-loadings were glum; all spring and summer and even into the fall, more volunteers than we'd known what to do with joined us for the weekly trips into Mexico. One day, we had over a hundred eager American kids loaded into buses ready to go forth and change the world. Now, though, as the late-winter/early-spring rain came, the group dwindled. Sometimes we were reduced to a small core of old-timers, six to ten at most.

When we pulled into the dump, the vans slid almost sideways in the viscous, slick mud. Windchill turned the air icy;

there was no smoke to speak of that day, and the dogs were mostly hiding. Women awaiting food were lined up, covering their heads with plastic sheets. Even in this wind and wet they joked and laughed. This feature of the Mexican personality is often the cause of much misunderstanding—that if Mexicans are so cheerful, then they certainly couldn't be hungry or ill. It leads to the myth of the quaint and jovial peasant with a lusty, Zorba-like love affair with life. Like the myth of the lazy Mexican, sleeping his life away, it's a lie.

Perhaps the women laughed because they were simply relieved to be getting food. Perhaps they were embarrassed—Mexicans are often shamed by accepting help of any kind. When embarrassed or ashamed, they often overcompensate, becoming boisterous, seemingly carefree. Or maybe the poor don't feel the compunction to play the humble and quiet role we assign them in our minds.

As I climbed out of the van, Doña Araceli, the Cheese Lady, bustled over to me. We called her the Cheese Lady because she had taken to coming to the dump with globs of drippy white goat cheese wrapped in cloth. She sold it to the locals, and she always pressed a lump of it into my hands as a gift. Nobody in the crew had the guts to taste it. We'd pass the cheese around for a couple of hours, then unload it at an orphanage or a *barrio* in Tijuana.

Doña Araceli was extremely agitated. She had discovered a new family—a married couple, several children, including toddlers, and one daughter with an infant—and they had no house to stay in. They were very poor, she said, and in dire need of help.

One of our projects over the years was to build homes and churches for the poor. An associate of ours named Aubrey devised an ingeniously simple construction plan. He collected garage doors from houses being torn down or renovated; these doors, hammered to a simple wooden frame, made handy walls. Depending on how many doors were available, the new house could be as long or as wide as the builders chose. With saws and donated windows, Aubrey could modify the place and make it quite fancy. The roofs were either more garage doors, ply-wood, or two-by-six planks covered with plastic sheeting that was either carpet-tacked or stapled into place. Old carpets and plastic sheets were transformed into a quick floor. Once a month, we had a *dompe* workday: truckloads of youths armed with tools came in and began hammering, and in a matter of hours, they created a new building.

Doña Araceli wanted us to build this family a house right away. She said the mother was waiting to meet me. The woman's name was Jesusita. Little Jesus.

Jesusita shook my hand and called me *"Hermano"*— "Brother."

This is not a common Mexican greeting; it is used among Protestants as a shorthand for "fellow Christian." A "real" Mex-ican would never resort to such Protestant language (though it is a habit for Mexicans to call each other " *'mano,"* which is short for "brother" but actually takes the place of "pal" or "dude." Mexican linguistics are a delicate and confusing art: *mano* also means "hand"). The poor, however, deal with missionaries and soon learn to use the more religious term freely. It is often a manipulative thing. They are hoping you will assume they are *"Hallelujahs,"* too, and give them more goods than the rest. Consequently, Jesusita's *"Hermano"* didn't move me. I paid it no heed.

What really caught my eye instead was her face. She was small, a round woman with gray hair and the kind of face that retains a hint of young beauty under layers of pain and comfortless years. Her eyes, nestled in laugh lines, were a light, nutbrown color. She smiled easily. She wound her hair in twin braids and pinned it to the top of her head, framing her face. She made me feel happy, absurdly pleased, as though she were a long-lost aunt who had appeared with a plate of cookies.

Over the next year, as we got to be friends, she lavished me with bear hugs. Her head fit easily beneath my chin. On the day I met her, though, she cried.

"*Hermano,*" she said, "*vinimos desde el sur, y no tenemos casa.*" (We came from the south, and we don't have a house.) "*Somos muchos, todos mis hijos, un nietito, y mi señor.*" (There are many of us, all my children, a little grandson, and my husband.)

"Help her, Luis!" cried Doña Araceli.

Jesusita's full name was María de Jesús. Mary of Jesus.

Requests for help were a constant; they were the rule. That Jesusita needed assistance didn't make her special, but something about her involved me right away. I suppose it is the thing we conveniently call "chemistry." Still, Jesusita was one face in a river of hundreds.

Everyone needed help. For example, there was the family recently arrived from near Guadalajara. They had no clothes except what they were wearing, and the children were so infected with scabies that their skin looked like old chewing gum. Scabies is a mange caused by a burrowing mite, a louse, that tunnels through your flesh, leaving eggs under your skin. You scratch and scratch, but can never quite get to the itch—the mites move in you at night. They like crotches and armpits.

Scabies victims claw themselves raw. The kids didn't understand what was wrong with them. They all slept together, and the mites could easily move from body to body. Their beds were full of these mites; their clothes and underwear were also infested. When we tried to explain what was causing their itch, they looked at us with disbelief and laughed.

The family was living in a shack on a hillside across the highway from the dump. It could be reached only after a long and confusing drive through crooked alleys and ridgetop dirt paths. Lean-tos thrown together by junkies and winos surrounded their shack. You could smell the booze and urine coming through the slats. There was a small goat tied to a stake in the dirt, and no lights brightened the neighborhood save for small fires and the occasional flashlight. The men's voices were thick; they cursed and broke glass in the dark. In the shack hid Socorro, the thirteen-year-old daughter. The men wanted her. They'd come out after dark and storm the house, trying to break through the doors and walls to get to her. When I went up there one night, waving my flashlight in the dust clouds, I could hear them outside Socorro's door, howling.

Clearly, the Guadalajarans needed a new house. Everywhere we turned, someone needed a new house. Jesusita's family would have to wait for theirs, though we committed to giving them assistance wherever it was possible. I told Jesusita to wait for us in her place down the hill, and we'd be down as soon as we could. She cried again and put her arms around me. *"Gracias, Luis,"* she said. *"Gracias, Hermano Luis."*

Fear

This is a record of a small event that happened on a typical spring day near the pig village.

I was unloading one of the vans—the huge Dodge we called "the White Elephant." Some of my friends were standing around the van with me—Doña Araceli, a Mixtec woman named Juanita, and a little girl named Negra. I noticed a woman standing in the distance, among the trash piles. I didn't recognize her. None of the dump people seemed to know her, either. We watched her lurch back and forth, spitting and waving her arms. She would occasionally glare at me, start toward me, then stop after a few steps and curse. Her face looked like a rubber mask: white creases and a red-slash mouth.

"Is she drunk?" said Juanita. I said something, no doubt a joke, and leaned into the van. I worked the box I was looking for free by shoving one of the heavy bags of beans out of the way. When I turned around, the woman was standing right beside me, staring into my face. She snarled.

I stumbled back from her. Her hair stood straight off her scalp as though she were taking a heavy charge of electricity through her feet. She was wheezing.

One of the women said, "She's crazy, *Hermano.*"

"Fuck you," she snapped. Her voice was deep, like a man's voice. "*Vete a la chingada.*"

She leaned toward me. "We know you," she said. "We know who you are. We know what you're doing."

I laughed nervously. "What?" I said.

"You'll pay for this."

I put down my box. "I don't understand," I said.

She began to rasp obscenities in her man's voice. "We *know* you. We'll get you."

She spun around and jerked away from us, very fast. She stumbled over rocks in the road, but kept moving, shouting all the time, "*¡Vas a ver!* You'll see! We'll get you. We'll stop you."

She paused in front of Pacha's house at the top of the hill, gesturing at me and yelling her strange threats. The hair at the back of my neck began to rise.

"Is she drunk?" Juanita repeated.

The woman threw her head back and screamed.

Pacha

Pacha had startling eyes. They had a kind of gold-green edge; they had yellow flecks, like the eyes of a cat. They slanted up the slightest bit. If she'd lived anywhere but the Tijuana garbage dump, her eyes would have seemed like a movie star's.

She lived with a thin, dark man named José. He called himself her husband, though he was not the father of her children. His face was craggy and his teeth long, hidden by a thick black mustache. When he talked to you, he'd bob his head and grin. When either of them laughed, they'd cover their mouths with their hands. They were pagans when they came north, of full Indian blood, and not used to church services or ministers. Their marriage ceremony was more personal and private—José moved into Pacha's bed. He became her mate, and he remained faithful to her. It was a simple agreement, as firm as a wolf's.

José liked Jesus very much. When Pastor Von and his workers visited his house, José always asked Von to pray for him. We put our arms around each other and Von prayed and I translated and José kept saying, "Thank you, Jesus, for listening to me." He cried.

Pacha wouldn't come to the vans to get food. She said it embarrassed her to be begging and fighting with all those other women. I made it a habit to save her out a box of goods, and after the crowds dissipated a bit, I would take it up to her.

Her home was on a slope that swept down into the dump; hers was a long, meandering shack with a low roof and uneven walls. The entire house was at an angle. José designed it this way so that the rain, when it came, would flow through the house, under their bed, and down the hill. He was very proud of his ingenuity: he had built one of the dump's best-engineered houses. Those who built below him, on flatland or in hollows, found themselves in puddles of mud all winter.

Their floor was a conglomeration of carpet pieces and stray linoleum squares. José and Pacha pressed them into wet soil. The exterior walls were board. The interior walls were cardboard, with an occasional bit of wood—fruit crates, barrel slats. They sealed the gaps with plastic sheeting.

They did have one luxury: a bed. It was quite odd to look through a door and see a big bed with an iron bedframe and headboard. Often a bed was the only thing people in the dumps owned that was worth anything. Except for televisions.

You'd see little black and white TV sets scattered through the dump. There was no electricity, but there were wrecked cars in the *yonkes* in the valleys. The men took the car batteries and hooked the TV sets to them. Sometimes the TVs were balanced on huge oil cans—rusted Pemex, Opec barrels—which, when filled with paper and dung or twigs, served as stoves.

Pacha didn't have a television, but she did have oil barrels: she cooked in one of them. The other she used to store water. It was full of mosquito larvae wiggling like tiny fish. Its water was the color of blood.

Pacha's eldest daughter offered to pay me to smuggle her across the border. She was pregnant—her husband had gone across the wire and never come back. She watched for him on a neighbor's television. I told her I couldn't do it.

On New Year's morning, she had her baby in the free clinic in Tijuana. The nurse took the infant and dunked it in a tub of icy water. It had a heart attack and died. It was a girl.

Pacha got pregnant next. Her belly stuck out far and hard, like a basketball, from her small body. When we arrived at the dump, she stood in front of her house with José, pointed at me and laughed. They laughed a lot. She was furious with me if I didn't come up the hill right away to see her kids.

José had hurt his back. He could barely stand, much less work, and the days were hard for Pacha and her kids. They all had to take the trash-picking poles and work the mounds, supporting José, who would give out after a few hours.

When I took them the food, I'd pat that huge stomach and shout, "What are you doing in there!" They would laugh, and she would scold me for waking him up. It was José's first child with her, the seal of their marriage.

One day, when we drove over the hill, a crowd was there, milling. It was hot—the flies had hatched, and were forming clouds that swept out of the trash like black dust devils. The rain had been over for months, and the deep heat was on. I glanced at Pacha's house—nobody in front. Then I saw an old pickup truck coming up the hill. José was in the back with a group of men. They held cloudy bottles by the necks.

I waved at him, but he just looked at me as the truck went by, no emotion at all on his face.

As we were unloading the vans, one of Pacha's girls came to me and put her hand on my arm. "Luis," she said, quietly. "Mama's baby died."

I stared at her.

"Don José just took him away in the truck. His head was too big. He was all black."

I asked her if it had been born here.

She shook her head. "Free clinic," she said.

She stood calmly, watching me. "Mama needs you," she said.

I didn't want to go up there.

It was a terrible charade: Pacha was blushing and overly polite, as though caught in an embarrassment. I was pleasant, as though we were having tea and crumpets at the Ritz. Everything felt brittle, ready to shatter. She wore baggy green stretch pants and stood holding a salvaged aluminum kitchen chair.

"Poor José," she said, looking off. It was very dark in the house, and it smelled of smoke. "Poor José. It hurt him so much."

That look as he drove past, drunk: where was Jesus now?

"The baby wouldn't come out," she said. She looked at her feet. "The doctor got up under my *chi-chis* and pushed on him after I tried for a few hours."

"He sat on your abdomen?"

She nodded. "*Sí*. They got up on my chest and shoved on me. And then the doctor had to get down there and pull me open because the baby was black and we were both dying." She swayed. I jumped up and took her arm, trying to get her into the chair. "It hurts," she said. She smiled. "It's hard to sit." I got her down. "They stuck iron inside me. They pulled him out with tools, and I'm scared because I'm fat down there. I'm still all fat." She couldn't look at me; she bowed her head. "It's hard and swollen and I can't touch it."

I told her not to move and ran down the hill to get Dave, a medical student who was working with us. He grabbed a flashlight and followed me up.

Pacha repeated her story; I translated.

He said, "Tell her to pull the pants tight against her crotch so I can see the swelling."

She did it. He bent close. It looked like she had grown a set of testicles. He whistled.

"Think it's a hernia?" he asked.

"I don't know. Could be." Many of the women in the dump get hernias that are never treated—I knew one woman who had one for fifteen years until she asked one of us to look at it.

Dave said, "Tell her I have to feel it."

I told Pacha. She just looked at me. Brown eyes flecked with gold. "Anything you say." She nodded.

"Is she all right?" Dave asked.

"Yeah."

He handled her very tenderly; she winced, sucked air. "Feels bad," he said.

She kept her eyes on my face.

"We have to get her pants off, buddy."

"Wonderful, Dave."

"Culturally?" he asked.

"A disaster."

One of my aunts, when she was pregnant, was attended to

by a male obstetrician. My uncle ordered him to stand outside a closed door—his nurse looked at my aunt and called out the details to him. My uncle hovered nearby to make sure there would be no outrage against her womanhood.

Dave stood there for a moment. "Too bad. We have to look."

"Pacha," I said. "The, ah, doctor needs to see it."

She nodded. She took her children outside and told them not to come back for a while. I held her hand and helped her into the bed.

José had designed a little paper alcove for the bed. Pictures of musicians, movie stars, and saints were pasted to the walls. A ragged curtain hung beside the bed for privacy.

"He was too big," she said, stretching out. "Too fat."

She worked the pants down around her hips. A strip of dirty elastic—perhaps torn out of an old girdle—was wrapped around her fallen belly to hold it up. She unwrapped herself. Her navel hung out like a fat thumb.

She undid some safety pins that held her underpants together. They were blue, lightly stained. A smell rose of warm bread and vinegar. Dave sat beside her. She stared into my eyes.

I looked away. I was embarrassed and nervous.

Dave handed me the flashlight and said, "Here. Illuminate it for me."

Her right side was thick and grotesque. The right labium was red. Bits of lint stuck to her. Every time he touched her, Pacha gasped.

"Blood," he said. "Tell her it's blood. No hernia." He smiled at her.

I translated.

She smiled a little bit, more with her eyes than her lips.

We put her to bed for several days—no more trash-picking. She needed to let the blood reabsorb. Dave gave her a battery of vitamins, some aspirin, put her on lots of fluids.

"*Ay, Luis,*" she said.

I stepped out of her home. The sky was black and brown—they were burning dogs at the end of the dump. It smelled like Hell. I took a deep breath and walked away.

Coffee

It was finally time to go down and see Jesusita.

We climbed into the four-wheel-drive Blazer and drove down the slippery hill. The dirt road was already so deep in mud that the truck couldn't make it. We had to abandon it and slog down. In places, the mud went higher than my knees.

Jesusita and some of her brood waited for us at the bottom of the hill. They led us to what seemed to be—for the dump, anyway—an especially luxurious house. It was a small American-style place with stucco walls and what appeared to be a real roof. It even had a porch. We were a little suspicious at first. The Cheese Lady had made such a fuss about this? Our opinions changed when we got inside. Half of the interior walls had fallen in, with the back walls sagging and open to the wind. The floor was raw, uncovered cement, and the whole house was awash in one or two inches of water. Only two areas remained recognizable as rooms. In what had clearly been a living room, on a sheet of plastic, were piled all of Jesusita's possessions—clothes, bundles—forming a small dry island. The family slept on this pile. The other room was a kitchen.

They had dragged the empty shell of a stove from the dump. A linoleum-and-aluminum table stood in the kitchen, too, with four unmatched chairs. On the counter, a few coffee cups, a pan, and the meager food supplies we had given Jesusita. Her husband arrived, took off his straw *vaquero* hat, shook our hands, and very formally and graciously invited us to sit and have a cup of coffee with him. He was an iron-backed man, not tall, but erect and strong; his hands were thick and solid as oak burls. He wore old cowboy boots and faded jeans and a white pearl-snap shirt. We learned that he was a horse-breaker from the interior of Mexico, a real cowboy who took pride in his talents.

Jesusita said, "He is the best horse-tamer in our region."

He shushed her—he never liked too much talk of home. His tightly curled hair was tinged gray and white. A small peppery mustache sketched itself across his upper lip. He referred to each of us as *"usted,"* the formal "you," and it was clear that he expected the same respect. The most lasting impression we took with us was one of dignity and pride.

Their children were remarkably attractive—several girls and two little boys. One of the girls, perhaps fifteen, had a baby. All their hair was shiny and black, and the girls wore it pulled back in loose ponytails.

Jesusita put wads of newspaper in the hollow stove and lit them. She heated water in the battered pan, and she made Nescafé instant coffee with it. It was clearly the last of their coffee, and she served it in four cups. We men sat at the table. Jesusita and the kids stood around us, watching us drink.

It was a lovely moment. The weak coffee, the formal and serious cowboy, the children, and Jesusita, hovering over us. She broke a small loaf of sweet bread into pieces and made us eat.

It was also a fearsome moment—the water was surely polluted, runoff from the miasma above. A great deal of disease infested the area from the constant flooding and the scattered bodies of dead animals. To refuse their hospitality would have been the ultimate insult, yet to eat and drink put us at risk. Von had the grim set in his lips that said, *Here we go again,* and with a glance at us, he took a sip. We drank. *"¡Ah!"* we exulted. *"¡Delicioso!"* Jesusita beamed. The cowboy nodded gravely, dipped his bit of sweet bread in his cup, and toasted us with it. Outside, the cold rain hammered down. Inside, we all shivered. We could find no way to get warm.

The Serranos

I first met the Serrano family on a Thursday. Halloween was coming. Several women told me there was a very dirty new family living out at the far end of the pig village. The children were sick, they said, and the mother—who was about to have a baby—was dying.

I walked out there, to where the Serranos had thrown together a small compound of stray boards and bedsprings. The roof was low—about three feet high—and I had to bend over to get inside. The only room of the house was a combination bedroom and kitchen. Its floor was dirt, and the room was dark and smoky. The smoke came from a little cook fire in the far corner, dangerously near the wooden wall. Some papers and a couple of pots rested on a cardboard mat in the dirt next to the fire. In the other three corners, pallets of rag and paper lay in the dirt: the beds.

Two boys and a little girl squatted in the dark. When they saw me, they started laughing. I said, "Come out here."

The little girl had an unusual name—Cervella (Ser-VEY-yah).

"Where's your father?" I asked.

The eldest boy shrugged.

They all giggled.

"Where's your mother?"

"Cagando." (Shitting.) "She does it all the time."

They all nodded.

"All day," Cervella said.

Her face was covered in smudges, but under the dirt I could see dense scabs, dark as steak. I couldn't figure out what they were; they looked like a combination of scabies and impetigo.

"What is this?" I asked, putting my finger on her cheek. She shrugged. I took her arm, turned the elbow out; there they were again. When I touched the edge of a scab, pale orange blood leaked out. "Does it hurt?"

Shrug. "Itches." Giggle.

They all looked past me. I turned around. Mrs. Serrano had appeared in a patch of tall weeds. She scared me to death.

She was a zombie, right out of an old Boris Karloff movie. Her skin was sallow and had the texture of hide, all criss-crossed with tiny X's in the thick flesh. Her eyes were black, but overlaid with a dullness that looked like a layer of dust—I wanted to wipe them off with my fingertips. Her mood was so flattened that it seemed agreeable and mindless; on her mouth, a loose-lipped grin and a constant exhalation of dank air. When she stood next to me, I could feel her fever radiating.

She was very pregnant.

"Are you Mrs. Serrano?" I asked.

"Serrano?" she said.

Pause.

"Where is your husband, Mrs. Serrano?"

Pause.

She moved a hand in the direction of the dump.

"What's wrong with your daughter?"

She smiled slowly, looking at the ground. "My daughter? There is something wrong with her." She laughed in slow motion.

I was baffled.

I put my hand on her forehead; it was dry as a skull, burning.

"I have dysentery," she said.

Someone coughed behind me. Mr. Serrano had arrived to see who was bothering his family. He was a hearty man with a hat and a drooping mustache. He gripped my hand and pumped it.

"Good to meet you!"

I told him his wife was seriously ill.

"I know it," he said. "Watch this." He grabbed her arm and pinched up a section of her skin. When he let it go, it stayed elevated, like clay, or a pinch of Silly Putty. A sign of severe dehydration. They call it "tenting."

"Está toda seca," he said. (She's all dry.)

"The baby?" I asked.

She laughed.

"Touch it," Mr. Serrano said.

I put my hand on her stomach. It was hard.

I brought them supplies from the vans: water, a quart of vitamin D milk, a pound of rice, a pound of beans, a large can of tuna, a large can of peaches, a large can of fruit cocktail, one dozen flour tortillas, corn, a can of Veg-All mixed vegetables, bread, a fresh chicken, and doughnuts for the kids. I told Mr. Serrano to keep her in bed and to pour fluids down her, and I'd be back the next day with Dave and a *gringo* doctor.

They both laughed. He kept rubbing his hand over his face, up to the hat, down over the chin.

The next day, when Dave and I returned with the doctor, Mrs. Serrano was sitting in the sun on a broken kitchen chair.

"I'm back," I said. "Remember I told you I'd come back?"

She didn't respond.

The doctor crouched before her and felt her stomach. He pulled up her lids, felt her brow, and took her pulse. He shook out his thermometer and put it in her mouth. She submitted to everything.

"Tell her I need a stool sample. Tell her I need to see some stool."

I told her. She got up and motioned for us to follow her. She led us to the south wall of the shack—the outside of the kitchen wall. The single sheet of plywood was also the wall of the pig-pen. And she had been leaning against it to go; bloody ropes and spatters of feces were all over the wall. We were standing in it. Dave cracked, "There's nothing like really getting into your work!" Our can of tuna simmered about six inches away from this mess.

"Doesn't she know anything about hygiene?" the doctor asked.

I translated.

"What is it?" she asked.

The doctor handed me a paper cup.

"Sample," he said.

———

He gave her Lomotil to stop the diarrhea. We gave her several jugs of Gatorade, more jugs of water, and some clothes.

Mr. Serrano, who had stood in the background during all this, came up to me and said, "Don't leave us a prescription."

I told him not to worry—we'd pay for it.

"No," he said. "We can't read. We won't know what we're getting." The doctor had given him a bottle of antibiotics, and Mr. Serrano held it up to me and said, "And you'd better tell me what this says, too, eh?"

Whatever Mrs. Serrano had, it was cured within a week or two because of one donated hour and some pale capsules the doctor prescribed. Within days, her eyes brightened, her skin turned tender, and her fever vanished. They moved the pigs away from the wall and went out into the weeds beside the dump to relieve themselves. In time, she had a healthy baby.

The Curandera's Curse

The Serranos' accents were peculiar, and I couldn't place them. After I had gotten to know him better, I asked Mr. Serrano. He said they'd come from *el sur* (the south).

We had been trying to treat Cervella's skin, but nothing worked. There were short periods of remission when the skin cleared, then the lumps returned. The scabs soon followed. I stood looking at her arms.

"We have a little Maya in us," Mr. Serrano said. The day was bright. We were beside his low front door.

"You know, *Hermano*," he continued, "you won't cure Cervella."

"Why not?"

"It's black magic."

In Mr. Serrano's homeland, near Yucatán, there lived a witch named Erlinda. She often worked as a *curandera* (healer woman), working her spells to help those who paid for medical attention—the area possessed few doctors, no public clinics, and certainly no hospitals. One way Erlinda healed people was to roll a raw egg on their bodies, over the afflicted area. She then broke the eggs into bowls—if the stuff inside had turned black, then the disease had been "sucked out."

Erlinda was embroiled in an unexplained feud with one of Mr. Serrano's kin. He did not know what started the fight, but he was not personally involved. One day, she appeared at his door, demanding money—568 pesos. Serrano didn't have it, and he told her so. She would not leave and became abusive, threatening him and his family. He physically ejected her from his plot of land, and she stood outside his little wood fence and put a curse on him.

That week, Cervella's aunt—Mrs. Serrano's sister—went into a swoon and died. They took her to a clinic in her last hours, but she never revived. The Serranos were terrified, unwilling to even leave their compound.

Then Cervella fell ill. It began with a fever, and the fever rose until she became delirious. She soon fell into a coma. Mr. Serrano bundled her up and carried her to the regional Red Cross station, but they couldn't break her fever. They kept her overnight.

Mr. Serrano, not knowing what else to do, went out to his land to work. In one corner, he found a small pyramid of stones. He took it apart and discovered a bundle of Cervella's clothes knotted up inside it. He rushed to the clinic, carried Cervella out, and took her to a missionary house in the jungle. There, he told me, they prayed over her, and she awoke.

It is possible that Mr. Serrano was telling me a whopper. However, he was crying as he told it.

"I swear to you, Luis," he said, "she woke up. And the fever?" He brushed his hands before his chest, as though flicking dust into the wind. "Gone."

The Serranos so feared Erlinda after this that they fled north, running until they ran out of country to run through. The last time I saw her, Cervella's arms were still lumpy, scabbed over, oozing blood.

Dompe workday, December: Steve Mierau and I were going to shacks in the pig village, visiting the families there. The crew was in the lower dump, hammering new houses together. We were alone. Mierau was a slim prairie liberal from Nebraska who had fallen into Mexico as if into a dream. Somehow, he had the misfortune of being promoted to second-in-command. He lived in a garage next to Von's trailer when he wasn't in Mexico.

Since we weren't expected, we were free of the usual crowds of hungry people. We could take in cartons of food to each family. The Serranos were at home, and as we walked out there, we heard a commotion. Mr. Serrano was hollering and laughing, running in circles with a broom. The boys were charging around his feet, whooping, and Cervella was shrieking and clapping her hands.

"What's this?" Steve said.

"Get him! Get him!" Cervella shouted.

Then I saw the rat.

It was a big dump rat, trapped between all of them, running in panicked circles. Everywhere it turned, a Serrano waited. Mr. Serrano repeatedly smashed the broom across its back. He finally cracked its spine, and it fell over, scrabbling in the dust. They all laughed.

The oldest boy knelt behind the rat. They crowded in.

Mr. Serrano said, "Good boy. Do it!"

The kid reached into his back pocket and withdrew a pair of wire cutters. He held the rat down with one hand and fitted the cutters over its snout. He began to cut its head off, centimeter by centimeter.

Steve and I backed away. Before we knew it, we were running for the van.

Corpses

Spring finally came, and the drive to Jesusita's house became more easy as the hills dried out. Her husband had not been able to find work, she said, but they had covered the biggest gaps in the walls, and they had settled into the house with a certain amount of comfort. Jesusita's husband was seldom there. "He's looking for a place with horses," she'd say.

He was the topic of gossip. Some people said he was a horse thief. This wasn't any big deal, especially in the dump. A boy who lived in the pig village had a pony that he'd stolen from one of the small ranches on the outskirts of Tijuana. He used the pony to rustle cattle from the same ranches. He fed his two brothers this way—their parents had disappeared—and he was quite proud of his outlaw status. He was thirteen when he started.

Something else about Jesusita's husband caused them all to talk. Crime wasn't it—crime would have made him something of a celebrity. Perhaps it was that stoic silence of his. His self-possession seemed arrogant, perhaps, and Mexicans hate an arrogant man.

They said he'd been involved in a major crime down south and had turned evidence against his accomplices. The rumors said he'd fled north with his family to escape reprisals—both from the criminals and the cops. Now that he was known to the police in the region, he'd be hounded continually, forced to set people up for arrest or worse . . . even innocent people.

Jesusita, on the other hand, seemed genuinely popular. She took part in the dump's church services, attended every event and Bible study. (They had their own church, and their own itinerant preacher.) She and Doña Araceli enjoyed a cordial relationship, and every time we came over the hill into the dump, the two of them barreled into me and lifted me off the ground. It became a regular practice for us to give her a ride down the canyon at the end of the day. The little boys would charge out from the house and play tag with me. One of them delighted in being captured and held upside down. They had gotten some pigs, and I was always ready to heap lavish praise on such fine hogs.

But one day, Jesusita told me she had to leave the house. They'd been fixing it up, planting some corn and expanding the little pigpen in the back. She insisted someone was making threats. We didn't believe her.

The next week, she directed us to the home of an old woman in the valley across from her house. Jesusita told me the woman owned the house and had threatened to harm her family if they didn't leave. Von and I went to the woman's house and talked to her. There was no problem, she insisted. They could stay. I was confused. Was Jesusita lying?

As we left, Jesusita held me hard and cried. "I'm afraid," she said. I would never see her again.

From the condition and location of the corpses, police pieced together this scenario: Jesusita and her husband were led up a canyon several miles from the dump (or taken by car to an abandoned stretch of road—I couldn't get clear details). At least two men accompanied them, and a small boy, possibly Jesusita's son—the same one who loved to be chased around the yard. The boy escaped. According to the testimony of the children, the men had appeared at the door and had seemed friendly. They told the family that there was a great deal of free lumber at a certain site. They said they knew of the family's troubles, and they wanted to offer their help. Jesusita and her husband went with them. They took the boy for extra help, thinking there would be a heavy load to carry.

Jesusita's husband was held by the arms, and a sawed-off shotgun was notched under his nose and fired. It blew his head to pieces, leaving only the back of his skull, with the ears attached.

This must have happened very quickly. Apparently, the shooter had his shotgun under a coat.

Jesusita and the boy ran. The child hid himself. The gunmen went after her. She was not fast—her legs were short, too short to carry her out of range. They shot her in the spine, knocking her facedown in the dirt. They must have taken their time reloading, because she managed to crawl a short distance, bleeding heavily. The shooter walked up to her, put the shotgun to the back of her head, and fired.

———

The next day, a note was stuck to the door of the house. It said: IF YOU ARE NOT GONE BY TOMORROW WE WILL COME AND KILL EACH ONE OF YOU.

The children scattered. They were gone when I got there, and they left no word about where they could be found.

Through the grapevine, I was told that if I was really interested in the shooting, one of the men would sell me the shotgun. It was going for forty dollars.

CHAPTER TWO

Negra

Negra was a tiny barefoot girl who had curly black hair and large, startling white teeth. She was so skinny that she was firm as wood; when you picked her up, you could feel her angular pelvis and the chicken-wing bones in her back. She was very dark, hence the name "Negra." In Spanish, it means "black girl." Her real name was Ana María.

I am not sure when I first met her. She just seemed to be there one day, moved into a shack with her mother and sister. Her father was gone; it was never completely clear where, though the obvious destination was clearly visible, about three miles to the north, being patrolled by helicopters. Like most people in the dump, she was from elsewhere—freshly arrived from Michoacán—part of an immigrant drive north that died out at the border, either from exhaustion, fear, or a sudden draining of vision and will.

It happens a hundred times a day—if you think the "illegal alien" problem is bad in San Diego, you should see what it's doing to Tijuana. The streets and *barrios* are swelled with nervous strangers from Sinaloa, Oaxaca, Chiapas, Yucatán, Quintana Roo. Then there are the actual illegals—Salvadorans fleeing death squads, Guatemalans fleeing the soaring poverty and crime of their homeland, Hondurans and Nicaraguans fleeing God knows what. Tijuana is like a dam, and it's beginning to groan before a tidal wave of human flesh.

Whenever we'd pull in, I'd look for her. Sometimes I'd hear my name being called very faintly, and I'd look up, and this kid would be hurtling through the trash, bare feet throwing up clouds of ash. Always the same dull dress, a kind of brown-gray. She'd leap into the air and fly into my arms like a bird. She usually smelled of smoke. She would be with me for the rest of the day, helping me give out food to the women, whispering secrets in my ear: her sister had a boyfriend, her mother had been in a fight, a boy from down the hill had walked her home. . . .

Negra was the one who taught me to pick trash. We'd take our poles and wade into the mounds. She wanted tin cans to sell for scrap, and any unbroken bottles were small treasures. Mari, Negra's older sister, was pregnant after a mysterious tryst with a dump-boy, and the occasional load of defective or water-damaged Pampers was a dangerously valuable find. We'd hide them under other trash on Negra's cart and hustle back to her shed. Of all the things one could take to the dump-dwellers, Pampers made the situation the most volatile. Imagine raising an infant with no diapers, no water, no baby powder, no baby wipes, no ointment for diaper rash, no formula, no money. We learned the hard way that the best way to start massive fistfights was to show up with a few boxes of Pampers: there is nothing so desperate as a mother fighting—literally—for her baby's ass.

They lived in a one-room shack, and in those days, there was no light. The two girls shared a bed, and their mother slept in another bed. Negra's brother lived with them, too, though he was never there. He attended school every day.

One day, near Christmas, I found Negra sulking with a cap on her head. Her mother had shaved her head. Her scalp had been invaded by a strange white flakiness, and great patches of it would peel off, taking hair with them. None of our salves worked, so her mother took a razor to her head, to "let the sun at it." I thought Negra would die of shame.

Negra wanted one thing in the world—a doll. "A big one," she said, "like a real baby."

Her mother told me, "She's never had one."

I had no money at the time. None. When not in Tijuana, I worked as a part-time tutor in a community college for roughly four hundred dollars a month. One of the students at the college overheard me talking about this poor girl with no Christmas, and surprised me a few days later with a thirty-dollar doll with real hair and blinking eyes. When Negra opened the package, she cried.

They made a little shrine for the doll in their house. Negra kept it up on a shelf, where she could look at it. She never took it out of the box. She didn't want the dust and ash of the dump to wreck her baby, so when she played with it, she'd have it in the box, still wrapped in plastic.

Negra had another problem: to go to school, she needed shoes.

All students in Mexican schools must wear uniforms. The idea behind this is noble: if everyone dresses exactly alike, then the middle-class kids will be no "better" than the poor kids. Everyone will be equal and have an equal chance.

In theory it works beautifully. Of course, the richer kids can wear new uniforms, new shirts and shoes. They can wear a new uniform every day of the week if they please. The poor kids must wear one uniform every day until it falls off; often they go home and wash their pants and shirts every night. And if they're really poor, they can't afford shoes. In Mexico, the bare foot is not a symbol of comfort—it is often a symbol of shame.

Negra had missed the opening of school, and she wanted to learn how to read and write. Her mother came to me and told me about it. She was surreptitious, because Negra was proud.

I invited Negra to come with me to downtown Tijuana. She piled into the van eagerly. We drove into town and shopped in

the shoe stores along Avenida Revolución. It was an incongruous sight—little ash-gray Negra, barefoot in the shiny glass-
and-chrome shoe store, watched over by yuppie Mexican
women in Jordache jeans and duty-free Parisian perfumes. The
saleswoman was gracious in the extreme, taking the measure of
Negra's feet and brushing the ashes off gently when she brought
out the shoes. We bought Negra black shoes, and with some
money to buy a uniform, she was able to attend school.

One day, on her way back home from classes, a gang of
barrio kids caught her, beat her up, and stole the shoes.

She had to wait two weeks until she saw me again. I immediately bought her a new pair, but when she got back to school,
they told her she had failed and been expelled. She had missed
too many classes.

It was a warm day in spring: we had pulled in with a huge
load of clothing and food. My mother and I had collected 150
half-gallon plastic jugs, and we'd been up at dawn in her backyard, filling them with the garden hose. I hadn't seen Negra for
two weeks. I wanted to get a box of food to her family before the
crush started. I took cans of corn, string beans, fruit; a sack of
pinto beans; a kilo of rice; several jugs of water; bags of doughnuts, bread, bananas, oranges, onions, avocados, and plums.

There were men gathered around Negra's shack, grinning at
me, then looking at their feet. I glanced in the door; an undulating shadow revealed itself to be a couple having sex in the dirt.
Negra's shack had become a whorehouse. Negra was gone.

CHAPTER THREE

Los Cementeros

His name was Andrés. He awakened with the sun. He lay in bed as long as he felt like it, picking the crust of glue off his upper lip. It was white and vague as milk, but hard; it pulled out his whiskers, which were few and thin, black against his dark brown skin. Bed was a mat of folded cardboard on the broken roof of what used to be a small house on a forgotten hill above downtown Tijuana.

A few years ago, the house burned and the city's services were cut off from the hilltop. The steep alley that led there was left to wash out and be broken up by weeds and grasses and small trees. You could pass the alley's mouth a hundred times and never know there was anything up there. All you'd see from the street was a carpet of shattered glass and clumps of trash. Besides, this was not near the main tourist routes of Tijuana. This was west of the main city, an area of tawdry used car-part shops and sidewalk clothing vendors.

If you paused at the alley's mouth at night, and if you looked up, you would see the far end of the slope backlit by streetlights beyond the summit. And in that glare, you would see indistinct movements: legs, and bodies nervously shifting. And if you were white, and they saw you, they would come swarming down on you in a pack—feral and hungry. And they would feed.

They were the *cementeros*, the glue addicts and paint-thinner sniffers who lived on that hill with Andrés. *Cementero* derives from the word for "glue," which is the same as the word for "cement": *cemento*. Literally, *cementero* could be said to mean something like "cementer," though it has a stronger connotation that is almost religious. *Cementeros* are "followers of the glue." (Aptly, and somewhat eerily, *cementero* is almost the same as the word for "cemetery"—*cementerio*.)

Their numbers were (and are) fluid. These homeless boys were thrown out or had run away. They had wandered into downtown Tijuana from violent homes or the shattered homes of downtown's hookers. They were the sons of the women who copulated with animals in the downstairs bars in the lower depths off Reforma and Revolución. Some of them were orphans, some of them had parents in jail.

They found each other. They formed small groups like street kids everywhere, and they thought they would engage in the utopian dream of cast-off children: they would look out for each other, form their own street version of the families they lost. But this was Tijuana. And the hustle of these streets left no time for utopias.

Daily life revolved around prostitution and drugs. Soon the boys realized that the thousands of *gringos* who came down to party on the weekends made easy targets—especially once they'd had enough to drink. The boys lured the tourists away from the disco lights. All it took was a promise: girls— *muchachas bonitas*. They were sly enough to know that we still believed the racist myth of *fock my seester,* and they said it. And the gringos followed.

Or they offered dope, cheap. Or themselves. Or watches. The point was to get the victim alone. Then the one boy magically became three, four. Eight arms, eight legs lashed out of the dark and pummeled, with fists, shoes, rocks, pipes.

This on a good night, when the boys were feeling kind. Every one of them carried a knife, or a sharpened screwdriver, or a jagged strip of metal. Andrés kept his tucked in the back of his pants. Sometimes one of the boys was just cranky, just feeling grouchy. So he sliced the drunk *gringo* for good measure.

Sooner or later, some of these boys found their way up the hill. Of course, it seemed a haven. It was like a fortress. They felt safe from other, meaner street toughs, the *cholos* and *surfos* (ersatz surfers, whose gang colors featured the bare footprints of Hang-Ten logos that were sometimes drawn on their baggy shorts with pens). And, as always, the police.

However, the hill had its own harsh rules. Every boy looked out for himself, and alliances were often more dangerous than loneliness. Everybody was distrusted.

On the night I first met Andrés, I was led up the alley by an ever fearless Von. All the other boys had heard us coming and vanished down the other side of the hill like rodents. They were soundless and invisible and gone before we were halfway up the hill.

Andrés stayed behind. I could see him, stark and stick-thin against the lights. He stayed behind because he had to—Andrés had two deformed knees that turned his feet perpetually sideways. He couldn't run. He couldn't even walk. He balanced on two aluminum crutches, and he moved slowly when he moved, his feet dragging and banging along the ground.

"Nobody looks out for nobody," he told me.

We were looking out at the city lights.

"Fucking lights," he said. "Beautiful, *¿qué no?*"

"How do you eat?"

He smiled. "Stealing." He acted out delivering a blow with his fist. He ducked his head like a little boy. *"You* know," he said.

Andrés was barely five feet tall. He had long hair, long graceful hands that looked delicate—painter's hands.

His clothing was old and dirty: baggy cords and three shirts, a grimy watch cap on his head. He wore battered Converse high-top basketball shoes on his tangled feet. The jaunty shoes made his feet seem small. Everything about him was evocative of a child. It was disconcerting, because he was saying, "We gang up on them and beat them up and steal all their stuff."

He had the features of a Mayan carving—slightly sloping forehead, large nose, turned-down mouth. His eyes were bright as obsidian chips.

"It's hard for me," he said. "I can't run. So I try to join in when they've got the guy down."

"Do you use your crutches?"

He laughed, covered his mouth with his hand.

"Sometimes," he said.

All over the hill, there were little burrows where the boys buried jars filled with money or watches. No one dared disturb another boy's jar, and when one was tampered with, the revenge was swift and final. They killed each other with stones or knives.

The violence attracted the infrequent attentions of the Tijuana police. The cops raided the hill sometimes and delivered their version of social service to the boys: sound beatings. "Torture," Andrés called it. To avoid the cops, or anybody else, the boys dug elaborate tunnels under the house. At the least hint of approaching feet, they dove into their rat mazes, where they hid, only their eyes peeking out from under the slab foundation. They slept under there, too, jammed in on top of each other in the cold. They had sex there, sometimes undulating against each other underground.

And, at all times, there was the glue.

They were reduced to shambling zombies by it, their brain cells melting inside their skulls to give them their escape. There were nights when the tunnels were jammed with mindless, drooling bodies; the boys shrieked in hallucinogenic terror under there, came charging out like enraged pit bulls, swinging their knives at ghosts. Then they passed out, arms flung open to the sky, which must have seemed a baffling wonder to them before they slipped away.

This was the best hour for murder. When a boy had a vendetta against another, he would choose this time of coma in which to strike. The most recent murder had involved two lovers. One of these two fell in love with a third. The new couple plotted to kill the old lover and take his jar. On the night of his last high, they waited until he'd fallen over, then they crushed his head with cement blocks.

"That's why I sleep on the roof," Andrés told us. "Nobody looks up there. They're always looking in the dirt."

We'd gathered at a street-side taco stand. We were buying him supper. It took Andrés about ten minutes to get down from the hill. I walked with him, while Von went ahead.

"What's wrong with your knees?" I'd asked him.

"I need surgery."

"Could you walk after it was done?"

"That's what they say," he said.

"How much does it cost?"

He blew air out through slack lips. "Oh. Forget it. Too much."

"How much?"

"Two hundred and fifty dollars," he said, shaking his head at the immensity of it.

We bought him a paper plate of tacos.

"I like gum," he said. "Do you have any bubble gum?"

I did.

He smiled.

As we left him, he reached out and took my hand. His fingers were soft and limp. His hand was cold.

"Be careful," he said.

The last I saw of him, he was balanced on his twin sticks, smiling a little over his plate of tacos and staring at us. He was smaller than everybody around him. And they repeatedly bumped into him as they passed, rocking him until it looked as though he were going to fall.

CHAPTER FOUR

Happy Birthday, Laura Patricia

Laura Patricia lived in San Antonio, a small village inland from the port city of Ensenada. The town was nothing much: two small stores that sold beer, mostly, and a scattering of whitewashed houses nestled in a bend in the road among small vineyards. We stopped there every two weeks on what was known as "the Long Run"—a three-hundred-mile haul that took us down the coast, then back northwest, across vast landscapes of mountains, high desert, and prairie.

In the early spring, the rains would be beginning to taper off. The floods of 1978 and '79 had devastated parts of the region. Bridges were cracked in half, and the town of Guadalupe had actually washed away, with nothing left but outskirts surrounding a wide mud flat. San Antonio itself was hit repeatedly by the creek that ran between it and the orphanage we visited on the run. During the worst rains, the creek swelled to a mad river for a night, rising over its banks and screaming through house after house, blowing out the windows in brown torrents.

Our job was to bathe kids, wash heads, deliver food, and attend to any minor medical crises we discovered at the orphanage. Laura Patricia lived in a small house behind the corner market and across the creek. When I met her, she was about ten —a pretty girl with copper hair. Neighborhood kids were allowed to go over to bathe and get shampoos after the orphans had finished.

Each child was awarded a treat bag for bathing—he or she got two doughnuts (day-olds donated by Winchell's), two or three pieces of fruit, and a carton of chocolate milk. We had reservations about the chocolate, but learned that the kids wouldn't drink plain milk. They'd often give it to the dogs.

Colored poker chips, won in competitions, "bought" sundries at a small "store" set up in the back of one of the vans. Orphanage boys always helped put together the treat bags—for a fee. They were terrors, but the prospect of being paid in chocolate doughnuts for their tireless efforts turned them into little Jimmy Swaggarts. They pontificated from the fruit table, strutting and exhorting the other kids to be as holy as they. We'd stuff over a hundred bags, and they'd eat at least as many chunks of doughnut.

In the background was Laura, watching.

Later, when I'd go out to work on heads and hair, she'd follow me. Finally, one day, I asked her if she'd like to help me wash. She immediately took over the rinse-and-brush brigade. I'd be raising a ruckus with the children: "Brace yourself, I'm going to pour hot soup on your head! Watch out—here comes a cup of hot coffee!" She would shake her head at me like a wife. Whenever I sat in a chair, she'd come into the house and sit near, not looking at me, as though it had been the sheerest happenstance that we were there at the same time. On rare occasions, she would sit on the arm of the chair and put her hand on my back.

Laura did not bathe with the other kids.

Her mother had breast cancer, and we often paid for her bus trips to Los Angeles, where she got her treatments. The chemicals made her bloat until she was unrecognizable, and they ultimately did little good. Her right breast was removed before we met.

Five years after her mother's first mastectomy, Laura turned eleven. She transformed from a quiet, moody little girl to being a tall, beautiful young woman. Her hair went long and wavy of its own accord, and her walk became graceful. Her body began to curve and lengthen. She remained quiet, though. Her thoughts and feelings were almost always a mystery.

Sometimes, when her mother had bad spells, Laura wrote to ask me for help in getting her to the hospital. One day, I got a letter telling me that she had to begin kidney dialysis; Laura was terrified. She asked me to get everyone to pray so she wouldn't die. Then she told me that the next time I saw her it would be her twelfth birthday. Her mother was going to give her a little party, and she wanted me to be the guest of honor.

A friend of mine gave me five dollars to give to Laura. I put it in her birthday card, along with twenty dollars from me.

Another Chicano friend of mine named Rico had been going down on the run with me. Rico was in the MEChA (Movimiento Estudiantil Chicano de Aztlán) organization at the college where I was working, and he had helped get some clothes collected for Tijuana. He had become somewhat of a cause célèbre with the Mexico Crew—he drove a chopped and severely modified low-rider VW bug. It had roses etched in its tiny windows, and "suicide doors"—they opened in the opposite direction from regular car doors. It also had a Porsche engine that made a violent racket. His license plates said QUE MALO. (How Bad.)

Rico was endearingly obscene. He'd be in the midst of a pack of Baptist Bible students, and when something startled him, he'd cry, "Jesus Christ!" or "Holy shit!"

Incredibly, his great charm seemed to make them deaf to his sins. The church folk swarmed to him. I often wondered if the Baptist sisters didn't dream they could tame the beast, make of him an upright Bible-believing missionary.

Rico's cry could always be heard in the distance: "Holy fuckin' shit!"

Rico piled into a van with me. When we got to San Antonio, it was drizzling. Laura was standing out in the dirt road, watching for us, alone. When she saw us coming, she ran inside.

There were actually two orphanages near Laura's house. The crew would pull into the first and begin the bathing. A small group moved on to the second, to begin preparing the food bags and washing heads. Rico, a woman named Diana, and I left the first crew and walked through San Antonio. When we got to Laura's house, she ran outside and took my hand. I slipped her the card and told her I was hoping she would buy her own gift, since I didn't know what to get her.

Von had given me a digital wristwatch for her, too, but I wanted to spring that on her later.

"You've got to come to the party!" she insisted.

"I will," I said.

"Bring your friends."

"All right," I said. I told her we were walking to the orphanage.

She walked along beside me, as quiet as always.

Between the village and the second orphanage, the stream had erased the road that once cut through its bed, so the government erected a stone bridge over it. This bridge took an age to build, and they didn't grade the ramps leading up to it. Within a couple of years, the soil had washed away from either end, leaving a nice stone sculpture of a bridge in the air.

We started across, looking down as we walked. The stream was still running with water from the rains, and we all paused on the stone bridge above it. The whole thing was clotted with tadpoles. The shallows were black with them, and they squirmed furiously in the water. I picked up a dirt clod. I wanted to drop it in one pool and separate the tadpoles to get an idea of how many there were. When the clod hit, the splash threw fistfuls of them onto the shore, where they thrashed.

"Oh shit!" Rico yelled. "You're killin' 'em!"

We barreled down the slope to the water's edge, on a tadpole rescue mission. Diana and Laura stood above us, laughing.

"Well," I said, "I can't let 'em die just because I did something stupid!"

"Right!" cried Rico. "Stupid!"

It took us about ten minutes to collect them all and get them back in the water.

We washed the heads of eighty kids that day.

When Diana, Rico, and I walked back to Laura's, it was misty. The air was a pale gray; the hills were invisible behind the gauze of water. Laura's mother had set a small table on the patio in front of the house. Everyone was waiting for Laura's uncle to arrive with Jell-O.

We were seated—I got the chair beside Laura's (she held my hand under the table), and Diana got a chair, too. Rico sat on a broken kerosene heater. I suddenly realized that was it. No one else was sitting with us.

Everybody fretted about that Jell-O.

Her mother brought out little bowls of chicken and potato salad, and she put a small plop of each on our plates. The neighbor kids pressed in around us and watched us eat, fascinated by the party. We ate the family's only food, and Laura's mother couldn't join us, nor could her friends. Laura was radiant. This was her big day.

In the background, I heard her mother mentioning *"tío"* (uncle) and *"el Jell-O."*

We tried to make the chicken last, but it was gone very fast.

Laura's mother cleared the table. She stalled as long as she could, and had apparently given up on the uncle. She hurried inside to get the cake when—suddenly!—the uncle appeared in a cloud of dust. The gathered kids rippled around us, excited. He leapt out of his car and threw a bowl of red Jell-O on the table.

Laura's mother brought out the cake. She had baked it there, in a paper-and-wood-burning oven. It was partially collapsed, and the yellow frosting was speckled with tiny black flakes of soot. The kids whispered as we cut the cake that they couldn't eat. Laura was smiling. I was about to take a bite when I glanced at Rico and Diana. They were silent, staring out at the drizzle. It was billowing, curtainlike, furling. We all sat there looking out. The small vines of the distant orchards clung to their white stakes; the red clay tiles of the tilemaker across the road lay on newspaper, soft in the wet. Dogs hunched together under trees like small herds of cows, trying to stay dry. Children all around us coughed.

Laura's fingers were cold and silky.

Diana's eyes slowly brimmed with tears; I watched them roll over the edge of her lower lids and fall. The whole world stilled around us. Rico looked at me. I looked at Laura's face. The cold had made pink spread across her cheeks. She was wearing perfume. On her face, there was the slightest of smiles. Nobody said a word. It began to rain.

CHAPTER FIVE

Good Friday

A boy named Sergio fell down and broke his wrist. He had been playing jump rope with a small group of kids, and they pulled the rope tight beneath him, catching his ankle and throwing him to the ground. His wrist twisted softly near his hand; he was pale gray with shock, and his skin was cold. His mother was not home, and we had to take him to town in one of our vans, looking for a clinic. Since this was Good Friday, most of Tijuana was locked up for the day—and many of the stores and offices would be closed all weekend. The one clinic we knew to be open was right around the corner, but it had a fearsome reputation in the neighborhood. Here, we call it allegations of malpractice. There, the people only had rumors: a boy with a broken arm had been taken in there by his mother. He was taken down the hall and put to sleep. When she was allowed to go back to him, an hour later, she was horrified to find his arm gone. They had amputated it.

We had Sergio lying on blankets in the back of the van; Sharleen, one of the faithful old-timers, held him in her arms. She had an ice pack pressed to his wrist, and she tried to steady him as we banged over the rough streets. Still, whenever we hit a pothole, I could hear Sergio groan. I kept directing the driver around corners, to all the *barrio* clinics and pharmacies I could remember, but they were all closed.

A massive Great Dane with a strangely mottled coat blocked the road. He was guarding the door of a pharmacy. Next door, we were thrilled to see a small clinic. It was open. The lichen-covered dog looked at us balefully as we dragged Sergio in.

The doctor's name, interestingly enough, was Dr. Virgen.

He looked at Sergio's wrist and said, "Bad break." He looked at it, felt it, looked in Sergio's eyes. All the while, Sergio whimpered incoherently. "I can do nothing without an X-ray," Dr. Virgen said. We couldn't budge him; a break like this could not be played with, and he was right. It was just that the town was shut down, and Sergio was getting worse. The doctor got on the phone and called around town. He found us a hospital in downtown Tijuana—it was open only for another hour. He repacked Sergio's wrist in ice and rubberized wrappings, and we sped off again.

When we carried Sergio into the hospital, the nurse took one look at him and said, "His wrist is broken!"

Sergio sagged sideways and vomited.

We were the last people out the door of the hospital. We got back to the Virgen Clinic, and the doctor looked at the X-ray, nodding. No matter what language they speak, it seems all doctors favor the same cryptic, stoic hemming and hawing and lip-pursing. They remind me of priests.

"I will set it," he said.

However, of course, there was a complication. Nobody had found Sergio's mother. There was no one to give consent to the medical work. "It's a problem," said the doctor. "You see, I have to put him under with an injection. If anything happens, you are acting as his guardian. It is conceivable that he could die. You are liable."

There wasn't really a choice. I told him to set it.

We took Sergio down the hall to the small operating room. I got him up on the table. "You okay?" I said.

He nodded, smiling weakly. "Look," he said, glancing past me.

I turned around. On the next table, slowly leaking blood,

was a mass of tissue. We stared at it. It was dense as a small sun, and we held to it with our eyes, afraid to ask what it was, or why it was there.

I sat in the echoing waiting room, waiting. It wasn't like an American doctor's office. No music played, for example. No framed prints of trout fishermen or mountain vistas. No magazines, and no cozy table lamps: the lighting was from tubes in the ceiling. There weren't even any carpets. You find very few carpets in Tijuana offices; most streets outside the center of town are either dirt or around the corner from dirt. There is no way for a carpet to survive. All the floors are linoleum. They have little more personality beyond that of a car wash.

The doctor came out and looked at me for a minute, cryptic to the end. "He's asleep," he said. "He'll be out for a few hours."

His nurse came out, then, putting on a jacket.

He said, "We're going out to dinner."

"What do you mean?"

"I'm taking my nurse to supper. I'd like you to watch my clinic for me while I'm gone."

I thought he was kidding.

"Don't worry," he said, "nothing could go wrong. We're closed for the day, and both patients are sleeping peacefully."

"*Both* patients?"

"Yes. We have a young woman in bed in the other recovery room. She's fine. If there is any trouble at all, the clerk in the pharmacy next door will assist you." He slipped on a jacket, saw his nurse out, and patted me on the arm as he left.

"*Gracias,*" he said.

————

Time dripped by. There was nothing to do. I went next door; a pretty girl was watching Tom y Jerry cartoons on Channel 12. She smiled at me and said, *"Qué curiosas las caricaturas."* (How curious—cute—these cartoons are.) I went back into the clinic.

Down the hall, Sergio slept. I walked to the other room and glanced in. All I could see was black hair. She was in bed, on her back, the sheet pulled up over her face. Her hair spread across the pillow. For a moment, I couldn't tell if she was alive or dead. Then I heard her take a breath, and another, almost silent in the darkness. I backed away from her door. I waited some more.

A gurney was parked in the hall. I lay on it, trying to take a nap. But Sergio and the woman made me too nervous to sleep. I walked into the small operating room, looking in the various drawers and trays, fingering the cold equipment. The tissue from the table top was now sitting in a Gerber baby food jar.

Magnetic curiosity drew me to it, though I was afraid to look. I tried to walk away, but found I couldn't leave the thing be; I had to look at it and figure it out. I picked up the jar— yellowish fluid, mixed with pale blood, swirled within. The flesh was red and gray, with tiny white blobs in it. Not horrible. Worse in the telling than in the seeing. I turned it over; plumes of blood curled against the glass.

I heard a sob.

The woman in the back room drew a hitching breath. I rushed to her door and stood, looking in at her. She had pulled the sheet down from her eyes, but she kept the rest of her face covered. Huge brown eyes with a thick fringe of black lashes. As I got closer, I could see the beads of her tears all across her bottom lashes.

Stupidly, I said, "Are you all right?"

She nodded.

"Can I help you?"

She shook her head.

"Would you like a drink of water?"

She shook her head.

"Do you need some Kleenex?"

She shook her head. Another sob. I was panicked, unable to help.

"Can I get you a blanket?" I offered.

She shook her head.

I stood there for another moment, then hurried from her room and ran over to the pharmacy. The girl looked up at me and smiled at me again. The television was blaring disco music. "She's crying!" I said. "The woman in the back room woke up, and she's crying. What do I do?"

The girl nodded. "Yes," she said. "She's sad."

I thought, *That's it?*

Finally, she said, "She's been sick. Her husband is at work, and we couldn't find him. Her mother's not at home. She's alone. She had a baby inside. It died in her, and *el doctor* had to take it out today. It's still back in the operating room, I think. They put it in a jar." She smiled reassuringly. "I think she's all right. She's just alone and sad."

I stepped to the window. Outside, a '68 Chevy Impala was running over a long-flattened cat. The cat was stiff, and its legs kicked as the car drove across its flanks—almost running, even in death. And the world seemed overwhelmingly dark to me that day. The young mother's sobs took root in my heart. They continue to grow there because on Good Friday I held her broken little savior in my hand with no reverence, only mild curiosity.

And come Easter, there would be no resurrection from the jar.

CHAPTER SIX

Pamplonada: A Fire in Tecate

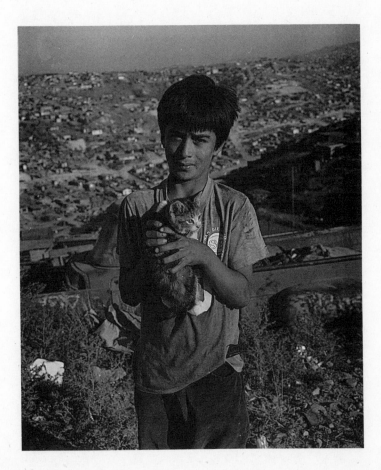

. . . not only underground are the minds of men
eaten by maggots.
—Antler

It was a noble experiment. For ten years, beginning in 1979, the town of Tecate, Baja California, sponsored a running of the bulls inspired by Hemingway's much-loved event in Pamplona, Spain. *Pamplonada* can be roughly translated as "Pamplonarama." Tecate is Tijuana's sweeter sister, a small border city that is mostly known as the home of Tecate beer. Most border towns have a twin on the other side, and Tecate is no exception. However, across the border, the hamlet of Tecate, California, U.S.A., consists of an evangelical center, a convenience store, and a parking lot. Down the road a bit, at Barret Junction, you can get some pretty good fried fish caught up in the reservoir.

Tecate is clearly not the sleazy and steamy border we hear about. When you consider that the border is two thousand miles long, it stands to reason that there can't be a Sodom in every port. Juárez and Tijuana have eternally stained the entire frontier. For example, if you head due east on I-8, you'll reach Calexico, California. Across the border is its twin, Mexicali. Mexicali is ugly, mean, dry, and hot—a town of rough *norteño* farmers and truck haulers trying to make a go of it in a desert. Aside from some dope hauls and the occasional gunplay, Mexicali has absolutely nothing to offer in the way of high-profile "border" excitement. Farther east is the Arizona city of Douglas, and its little sister, Agua Prieta (Dark Water). Low-key.

Believing that an adventurous event would attract *gringos* and enliven Tecate's somnambulistic reputation, the town fathers chose the running of the bulls as a sure thing. It was doomed from the start. Not only is the Mexican border not

Spain, but a hundred thousand drunk sailors, bikers, cowboys, and college kids is no army of Hemingways. The story of one of the last Pamplonadas reveals what went wrong.

The pace is slow in Tecate, and the people are more friendly than in the big city. The small park in the middle of town is furnished with a tiled gazebo. The city fathers have rigged it with speakers that play music all day for the folks who loiter on the benches. Tecate is a rural town, built in a hilly region long thought by local Indians to hold mystical powers. One conical hill nearby is greatly loved by UFO aficionados. Just south of town, past the Tecate beer plant, a small river floods in winter and blocks access to the main street, frustrating ranchers in souped-up pickup trucks.

During the Pamplonada, this bucolic scene is fractured by an army of *gringos* from San Diego and Los Angeles and swarms of louts from Tijuana and Mexicali. The prospect of seeing hundreds of drunks being pursued by angry bulls really appealed to me. The year before, an American had actually died (anti-climactically, from a heart attack), and street legend was full of unimaginably ferocious gorings and tramplings.

Evidence suggests that the bulls were in as much danger as the runners. On the same day that hapless *gringo* died, runners were seen ganging up on the bulls, kicking their legs out from under them and dog-piling on them. (As it turned out, the bulls were mostly rangy little yearlings.) A couple of the bulls were kicked silly, and the drunks branded them with cigarettes.

In an interesting twist, the organizers of the Pamplonada had decided in favor of the animals: for their protection, only older, larger bulls would run. That did it—I was going, and I was rooting for the bulls.

Friday, August 14

I was with my wild-eyed American friend, Mike, who had been living at an orphanage south of Tecate. We drove from Tijuana along the Mexican route—a two-lane highway that skirts the border and meanders through attractive backlands full of farms spread over low green hills. When we pulled into Tecate, a thin pale rainbow stood straight up from the brewery.

An orphanage in the interior had invited us to stay with them. It was one of my favorite spots in the world—a wide valley nestled between mountains and high desert hills, with a sprawling orphanage compound on a small farm tucked between a usually dry river and a cattle ranch. The property was once the site of an ancient Indian village, and prehistoric grinding stones could still be seen, bowls worn into the sides of boulders.

The kids knew where to dig for artifacts. One boy showed me some pieces of clay pottery. "Can you find some pieces for me?" I asked.

"Sure," he said. "Will you pay me for it?"

"How much?"

"A dollar."

I gave him the money, and he ran up the hill. In about a half hour, he returned with a coffee can full of fragments.

Less remarkable, but still of interest: a blue Ford Falcon station wagon half buried in the riverbed. The left front fender, half of the grille, and the driver's side of the windshield stuck out of the sand at an angle. One of the winter floods had dragged it out of the back country and buried it with powerful disdain. There used to be a small house near this site, but the river had washed it away.

As we drove through the orphanage gates, the children stormed out of their building. Their eternal struggle with American names was evident as they shouted, "Mai! Mai!" Night was falling. Mike settled down and cooked chili in his van. The children went back inside to eat their supper. I could hear them saying grace. A group of Americans was camping above the orphanage.

When Mike and I were ready to eat our chili, two of the older orphan girls stood outside the van with a tape recorder, playing tapes of Mexican ballads for us and singing along with them.

Later.

I sat in one of Mike's lawn chairs under a light pole, bare feet in the gravel, digging with my toes. Immense black ants sauntered across my feet, pushing the hairs around. Some of the *gringo* kids wandered around the farm in groups, afraid to brave the night alone.

A bunch of them collected at the leaky pipe near the chicken coops (where the boys kept ducks, too, and a pair of baby hawks, and an exhausted little rattlesnake). They went crazy every time one of the insatiable desert bugs got them:

"Ow! I just got bit!"

"Prob'ly a scorpion."

"*Ow!*"

"Not again!"

"Yeah! Like six times! It's *all over me!*"

"Is it, like, *flying*, or . . . *crawling?*"

Ironically, within the hour, one of their chaperones—the wife of their pastor—stepped on a scorpion and received a very painful surprise.

A fantastic tilework of dark clouds, backlit by a full moon, spread across the high desert like a disk, a hinged lid closing. The light atop the pole was attracting a swirling ball of desperate moths, crane flies, mosquitoes, and other frantic night fliers. From far off, I could hear—or, more than hear, feel—the *ping* and *tsch-tsch* of bats homing in on the insects. They dove into the globes of light and pulled straight out in stunning vertical power climbs.

This miracle was going on about ten feet above my head. The American kids never saw it. In the blue-gray haze of moonlight, the windmill looked capable of flight, a ragged gyrocopter on stilts. The clouds thinned out, and the moon seemed to pop through them, hanging beneath them, about a mile above the valley.

Saturday, August 15

We all rose to the million jangling sounds of a farm at dawn—cowbells and barking dogs, the arguments of crows and the mindless rusty squawk of roosters. A frog the size of my thumbnail policed the area, then flashed down a crack.

José, one of the orphans, sang "Sugar, Sugar" as loud as he could. That he didn't know a word of English didn't stop him:

CHOOGAR,
Da-da-da, da-DAN-DAN,
O honi honi,
Jou arr mine CANDOOL-GART!
Ah jou gommi A-WANNAJOU!!!

Driving toward Tecate, we saw a woman walking on the shoulder of the road. She was carrying the tiniest of babies, shielding it from the sun with a square of white cardboard.

Tecate, in the park.

Porta-Johns stood like a stockade around the edge of the grass. The runners were registered by age and gender: WOMEN, 20–25; MEN, 25–30, and so on. Drunks were already picking fights—a fat *vato* in mirror shades shouted, "You scared of me? Are you scared of me?"

Americans everywhere.

"I don't think this picture'll come out."

"Sure it will."

"I don't think so."

"Sure it will."

"You think so?"

"Sure."

"Okay!"

A man without fingers on either hand sold rubber joke items out of a suitcase—green dog turds, whoopi-cushions, small rubber chickens, bloody rubber thumbs. What did he think of when he sold these? Did he remember his own thumbs? Did he hate his customers and long after their fingers? Did he wish they'd leave their fingers in his case?

The lines at the toilets were long, but not unmanageable. A slightly disheveled Mexican man in his thirties, unshaven, shirt half untucked, cruised down the sidewalk and stopped to look at the lines of *gringos* waiting patiently to get to the toilets. He started to walk by, but did a double take. In retrospect, I believe this was where the idea hit. A stroke of genius so fast, so sharp, that at first I wasn't sure I was seeing it.

As soon as there was a slight lull in the pressing of the crowd, he stationed himself before the door of one toilet. When the next tourist stepped up, he extended his hand officiously, palm up, and wiggled his fingers. The startled American didn't protest—he dug out a quarter, and the Mexican opened the door and ushered him in. This ploy worked time and again. The man grew so bold that whenever the people within seemed to be dawdling, he pounded on the door and scolded them. When one of the passing cops slowed to look at him, the Mexican hustled his last customer out of the stall and locked himself in. He must have made a fortune that weekend.

Some charming friends of the orphanage named Socorro and Pepe lived in Tecate. Pepe was a huge man, with a walrus mustache. Socorro was dark and slender. Their daughter was named Yoloxochitl—a Nahuatl word for "Flower of the North." Socorro insisted we eat lunch with them, saying, "This is God's house. People know when they come here that they are home."

Over lunch, Pepe told me stories of Pamplonadas past. One year, he said, the lines to get into the toilets were too long, and one of the American women startled the Mexicans by dropping her pants and urinating in the street. Also, a friend of theirs walking with her mother was cornered by a group of American men who then fondled her, trying to pull off her clothes. I asked him what the Mexicans thought about *gringos* after such displays.

He pursed his lips. This was a sure sign of approaching diplomacy.

"We all know," he crooned, "that only your lower classes do such things."

I looked at him.

"The problem," he continued, "is that people are starting to think that all Americans are like this."

Yes, but what do people really think?

"*Gringos,*" Pepe said, "act like they've been in a box all year. Crossing the border makes them think they have an excuse to run wild. But you know what? I can complain all I want. If you were to ask a merchant out there about the Pamplonada, he'd say it was the greatest thing to ever happen to us."

That night, back at the orphanage, a bright thing sat above the horizon, glowing like a fat copper star. It pulsed on and off, then vanished. When I looked again, it was back, drifting north. I felt like one of those UFO ladies on cable TV, wearing their foil caps, chanting the aliens down.

The children engaged in the tumultuous process called "ready for bed." The oldest boy in the orphanage had the unenviable duty of foot patrol. He had to check all the orphans' feet to make sure they were clean and didn't get their beds stinky. When he found dirty feet, his wrath was understandably fearsome.

The kids were a little high: that day, the visitors had provided them with a *piñata.* One of the girls, an immensely fat kid named Carmen, paraded around announcing that she had collected exactly 182 pieces of candy. Several bruised and battered boys had made the sad mistake of trying to outrace her. She clutched the candies to her gut like the highest icons of the greed religion.

Suddenly, quiet.

Silence always descends like this in the back country. It's like a curtain that drifts over the scene, and there is an instant peace. The sound of an old truck grunted up from the valley, and at my feet, a massive stinkbug: the sound could have been his engine, grinding through the gears.

Sunday, August 16

Drinking coffee in Pepe's house. All the heavy traffic bound from Tijuana to Mexicali was rerouted down Pepe's street to free the main drag for the bull run. Periodically, conversation halted, battered into silence by the roar of big trucks. Some local businessmen stopped by to visit Pepe. One of them lit a cigar that looked like an immense cocoon, the pupating grub of some noxious prehistoric insect. He blew curling smoke all over the room. Yolo and Socorro suddenly commented on how hot the day had gotten. They bustled out of the room and, after some melodic rattling in a closet, reappeared with a tall fan. They plugged it in and turned it on. It was aimed directly at the cigar. Everybody smiled.

Mike and I began the day at the orphanage's prayer service, led by the farmer's wife. Though he is officially the director, she runs the place and directs the religious activities. While she preached, he milked the cows.

After breakfast, I found him in the kitchen, pouring the fresh milk into pails, straining the curds out with a cheesecloth.

"Buenos días, Don Victor," I said.

He nodded, offering me a clot of pale curd. "Have some!" he said.

"Is it good?" I asked.

"Well," he said, "it makes a good laxative."

We laughed.

We drank the milk and ate animal crackers.

Paramedics pulled in to Tecate from Tijuana, Ensenada, and Mexicali. Their blocky ambulances lurked at all the side streets. A double fence of steel bars ran down the center of the main street, Calle Juárez, forming a metal corridor to hold in the bulls and the runners. Plenty of room gaped underneath for people to dive out. A wooden bridge for TV cameras and the press spanned the run.

I could hear the unmistakable sound of a Mexican marching band: sqwonking trumpets not quite in sync with the tubas, and the drums keeping time to a tune of their own. It was time for the parade. The sound was deafening. A surfer next to me said, "Cheeziz Crize!" And the parade was upon us. Men wore hats made out of beer cans; one of them simply wore a beer carton over his head. Clowns, cops, mariachis. A Mexican motorcycle gang sat astride their hogs in full colors. "Los Vagos, MC— MEXICALI." (*Vago* means "vagrant," "tramp," "wanderer," "loiterer." However, among Mexican hard guys, to be a *vago* is to be *macho*. It's like being a human alley cat. Since this is Mexico, the Spanglish version implies another meaning— "vague.")

Suddenly, panic! The Club of Spain's float was taller than the press bridge. The entire parade came to a halt when the turret of the papier-mâché castle banged into it. The float's engine raced, then died. Very Important Officials followed their stomachs around, shouting orders.

———

Pepe and I discovered a snake charmer.

"Damas y caballeros" (Dames and horsemen, literally), "this serpent is the only serpent on earth trained to do card tricks!"

"This looks good," I said.

"Ladies and gentlemen, you will see my works! I don't ask you for money—I don't care about money! I am not a witch, I am a parapsychologist!"

Pepe guffawed.

The snake charmer pointed to a box. "Within, the deadly boa constrictor. An educated serpent!" He pulled the snake from the box—an apathetic four-footer—and waved it at the crowd. Girls jumped back; drunks called insults.

"Money?" he insisted. "I don't need money! If you have it, praise God! It was hard to earn!"

Pepe whispered, "Watch your wallet. These guys have partners who go around the crowd picking pockets."

"Do you comprehend what I'm doing?" cried the parapsychologist.

"Talking too much!" one of the drunks shouted back.

"You in a big hurry?" snapped the snake charmer. "If you are, then leave! This is a street. You can walk on it!"

He revealed his secret: he had a magic and sacred Rosicrucian cross made of parapsychologically effective magnets. For only twenty-nine dollars—U.S. cash money—we could have the very same special powers as he. The only power he was demonstrating, though, was a fabulous gift for b.s.

As we walked away, he was yelling, "I will now show you a card trick invented by the one and only ruler of planet earth—Napoleon Bonaparte!"

————

Pepe is a Charismatic Catholic. This new movement in the Mother Church combines the traditional Catholic Mass with Pentecostal (or Charismatic) excitement borrowed from the Protestants. Their Masses have both folk guitars and priests, the classic Liturgy and cries of "Amen!" and *"¡Gloria a Dios!"*— with eager arms thrown wide to the sky in order to receive the Holy Ghost. Although Mass is no longer said in Latin, Charismatic services offer an assortment of other "tongues"—a sweeping spiritual flame of babbling that is supposedly ancient Hebrew or Aramaic or the Language of the Angels. It sounds like "Habballa-babballa! Om-betta-bubballa!"

Like his faith, Pepe continually amazed me. At one point, he opened his wallet and whipped out a microfilm square with the entire Bible printed on it. It measured two inches by two inches. "English or Spanish?" I asked.

He looked stricken. "Uh . . ." he said.

As we walked, he asked, "How do you feel about smoking?"

"I don't do it."

"Yes, but what do you *think* of it?"

"It's bad for your health?" I offered.

Exasperated, he said, "Yeah, yeah. But do you think it's a *sin?*"

"No . . ."

"Good!" he sighed, pulling a pack of Camels from his pocket.

Pepe went home. I went back into the park. Recumbent bodies formed a colorful crosshatch on the ground. Words rose like bits of meat in boiling soup—"I take your picture?" "More beer, dude!" *"¡Mámi, mira la bomba!"* (Mommy, look at the balloon!)

A thousand registered runners crowded the bull run, joking, limbering up like joggers on a track. I squeezed through knots of people, working my way between the back of an ambulance and the steel fence. I was about a foot from some of the runners. They were talking big, acting fearless. The ambulance crew stood on the back bumper, their rig's doors open. They leaned on the top rail. I stuck my head through the bars and craned to see down the run: solid bodies.

A string of firecrackers exploded like a little machine gun, and a surge went through the crowd. The runners giggled. Then a cannon blast. A roar rose at the far end of the run, growing louder and louder as it rolled toward us, underscored by the sound of pounding feet. The runner in front of me turned to look, glazed over for an instant, shouted "Oh my God!" and scrambled up the fence, eyes screwed shut.

The bulls were almost too fast to see. They sped by in a blur of horn and flank. One man tried to grab a bull and was tossed aside, bouncing off the rails and back to the ground. The ambulance crew from across the street rushed in and put him on a stretcher.

About a block away, at a five-and-ten store directly behind the grandstand, a bunch of people had climbed on the roof, hoping to get a better look. Smoke began to snake up behind them. The street was still full of antsy runners, waiting for a second charge. The smoke blew across the roof and enveloped the people up there. They scrambled, trying to get off without breaking their necks. We watched the smoke rise. "That building's burning," I said.

One of the ambulance crew said, "The taco stand next door caught fire."

A breeze caught the smoke and looped it down into the

grandstand and over the runners. They churned. We heard a dull, repetitive thudding.

The crew chief said, "Something in the store's blowing up."

Sirens wailed, the lights on top of the trucks and ambulances jumped to life. The crowd, instead of dispersing, seemed to clench, to draw tighter. I couldn't move. The air stank of sweat, smoke, excrement from the bulls. A man near me vomited; a group of men cheered him and applauded. Crashing glass. A voice crackled from a loudspeaker: "Do not panic. Remain calm. Stay away from the area." *Stay away?* We were jammed right into it. The smoke had turned chemical, burning my eyes.

Two establishments caught fire—the store and the taco stand. Then the house behind them. No one had the keys to unlock the bars of the gates in the street, so the fire trucks couldn't get down the block to the flames. I helped a cop crawl through the fence.

Loudspeaker: "Please clear the area. Move away. You are in danger. Get your children away."

I followed the cop, watched him pull a woman out of the smoke; she was limp. The ambulance I was with couldn't move. They hauled her through the bodies, and as they lifted her, the last thing I heard the driver say before I lost track of them was "We'll have to lay her on the roof."

A gang of drunken *vatos* marched through, elbowing people out of the way, chanting, "Tecate's burning down! Tecate's burning down!"

The cop had vanished in the smoke. Whistles bleated, cans crunched underfoot. A bottle flew over my head and broke in front of me. I climbed through the fence on the other side, and I saw a man propped up against a pillar. His face was burned. One of the fire fighters draped a gooey white cloth over his eyes.

Loudspeaker: "There are propane tanks in the store. You must move at least two blocks away."

Mike ran up to me with a camera. "I'm taking pictures!" he shouted, diving into the smoke.

A cop came up to me, watched me write notes. "Press?" he demanded.

Instead of answering, I asked, "Officer, how did it start?"

He puffed up, hands on hips. "This is not known," he said. *(Esto no se sabe.)*

The nephew of the store owner ran up to us. He grabbed my arm. "Americans threw matches!" he cried, then ran back to the store. Another man passing by said, "Four dead."

"No!" the cop said to me very intently. "No dead. *No hay muertos.*"

There was no way to know if anyone was hurt or not. In fact, later that evening at Pepe's house, we watched the whole thing over again on the San Diego news. They reported a quaint and boisterous day with a cute little fire. It was pretty entertaining and benign, yet we had seen burned people being carried away. They were taken down the block and into an alley, the mouth of which was blocked off by police. There was also much talk on the street of a woman badly burned and carried away in a blanket. "It makes you wonder," I said, "if they were in the same city." Pepe turned off the TV.

Back at the fire, a group of *gringo* college boys stood next to the Mexican firemen, wrestling with hoses.

The store owners—I saw the nephew in there—tossed

clothes out through the broken plate-glass window, trying to save them from the water and smoke. Spectators ran to the window, punching each other, fighting over the T-shirts. One drunk man challenged every male to a fight, calling him *"¡Pinche buey!"* (Fucking water buffalo!) I was astounded to see a woman come through the crowd with a video camera on her shoulder. Her English-accented voice narrated into the mike: "They don't want to leave, the people begging for a thrill." Behind her came a woman wearing a red satin baseball cap with devil horns on it. On a nearby roof, speakers hummed and buzzed, then blasted Bill Haley's "Rock Around the Clock."

I stood in the flow, writing, being jostled. Suddenly, a man ran past me, pursued by police. They caught up to him about ten feet from me and bludgeoned him to the ground. People cheered them on. The man began to scream; the sound scratched down my spine. The street was full of violence. We were hysterical as chimps, throwing punches at anyone who came too close.

Then, as quickly as it began, it was over. The whole thing collapsed in on itself, and I found myself in the park, sitting on the fountain, hanging my head. Exhausted people lay scattered everywhere, sleeping the fire off as though it were a huge meal.

The cops stood around in huge groups, eating little vanilla ice cream cones.

One skinny officer told his pals about a drunk American woman he'd caught taking her clothes off in the street. She was a redhead. He said he told her to stop, but she refused. He said, "I told her, if you want to put on a show" (he said the word in English: *un* show), "I'll lock you in a truck with a bunch of my boys, and then you'll *really* have a show! Otherwise, get off the street!"

They laughed.

Kids were playing with foam-rubber lizards attached to straightened coat hangers. The little beasts swirled around our legs, in between the cops' feet.

An officer, listening to a walkie-talkie, jumped to his feet and shouted, "*¡Un treintaisiete!*" (A thirty-seven!)

They stampeded across the park. There I was, running in the middle of about a hundred Mexican cops. They scolded the stragglers: "Hurry up! A thirty-seven!"

We arrived at the scene.

Two cops were hustling a shirtless Mexican out of the crowd. They had his arms twisted up behind him. It hurt—he was up on his tiptoes. Two American women came after, being held tightly by grim female officers.

One of them shouted, "Oh God! Don't fight! Take my hand!" She was trying to reach back to her friend.

Her friend was too busy to notice. "Don't I have any say in this?" she demanded. The cop acted deaf.

"Don't fight them!"

The mass of cops followed in a tan wave.

I ran around them and caught up to the women as they exited the park. The second one shouted into a male cop's face, "No fuck! What the fuck do you mean, *no fuck!*"

The skinny cop from before nodded at me. "She was putting on *un* show," he said.

Mike found a kitten on a window ledge beside the fire. Someone had put him up there, and he was too small to jump down. He'd taken the brunt of the spray from the fire hoses, which probably saved him from burning to death. However, his nose was cooked, and his throat was so wrecked from the smoke and from screaming that he had no voice left. The smoke had made his eyes leak goo, and they were glued shut. I dipped my handkerchief in water and wiped them clean, but they filled up again. I wrapped him in my T-shirt. He gripped my knuckles with his tiny claws and purred.

Socorro cooked us a huge supper.

As we left, Pepe said, "Most people call this thing a 'Pamlonada,' but I call it a 'Simplonada.' " (This was quite a joke—*simplón* means "idiot." *Simple* means "simple," as in "stupid." *Nada* means "nothing." And, of course, the suffix -*nada* is similar to "-arama.")

I held the kitten in my lap as Mike and I drove out of town and up the hills toward the orphanage. We pulled in at Los Encinos to watch a country dance. Somber cowboys shuffled slowly around an open concrete slab with girls in hand-sewn dresses. Booths hung in paper streamers sold tacos and fruit. Paper lanterns wobbled in the breeze. During the fast songs, the ranchers clomped their boot heels, arms aflap like crows.

Monday, August 17

The kids woke me up at six. They wanted to know all about the Pamplonada. They loved the ugly little kitten, and they carried him around like a baby. He was still voiceless and blind, but his purr was startlingly loud. One of the girls got so excited that she danced all around me, inadvertently kicking my big toenail loose. We all stood there watching my foot squirt blood.

Don Victor wouldn't take the cat. He said he'd drown it if we left it with him.

Mike and I named the cat Bruce Springsteen, a Cat from the Street. We tucked him in my T-shirt inside a cardboard box and took him with us.

About fifteen arduous miles outside of Tijuana, we passed an old man struggling along the roadside on crutches. Plastic sacks of junk hung off the handgrips. We pulled over. I got out and helped him get in the van.

"Where are you going?" I asked.

"Tijuana."

"Where in Tijuana?"

"Tijuana."

I shrugged at Mike. The old man sat still, staring out the windshield as though he were driving.

"Tijuana it is," said Mike, getting back on the road.

The old man was dirty. He wore a pinstriped jacket, stained slacks, and several layers of shirts. On his head was a battered straw hat with a dove feather in the hatband. It was quite hot, but he wasn't sweating. He had tied rags around the handgrips of the crutches. He smelled like turpentine. His skin was so dark it was almost black.

"Bus station," he said.

At the corner near the station, I helped him out. I hung his bags back on his crutches. I tried to give him some water, but he refused it. I pointed him toward the entrance. He balanced himself on the twin sticks and moved away, never looking back. Not a word.

———

We expected trouble with the border guards over Bruce. I was half considering hiding him—he would have almost fit in my pocket. He kept his nails hooked in my skin, even in sleep, and purred constantly. He was very weak, though I had been able to get a little milk down him.

We finally decided just to be honest and show them the cat. We were lucky; the guard was a young woman who took pity on Bruce. She came around and petted him, and said, "Poor little thing." She even gave me some tips on trying to revive him before she sent us across.

We traveled 370 miles that weekend. When I got home, I had enough time to feed Bruce warm milk with a spoon, then tuck him in a box full of underwear. Von was waiting for me—it was time to go to Tijuana.

Wednesday, August 19

Two days later, little Bruce went to sleep and never woke up. He purred as he died. I buried him under the bushes in my backyard. I planned to take it easy the next day: it would be my birthday.

CHAPTER SEVEN

TIJUANA COP

He flicked on the siren. It whooped satisfactorily, sounding like a television show. *"Muévete, pendejo"* (Move, asshole), he muttered to the cars that blocked his way as he maneuvered the Río de Tijuana thoroughfare. I glanced at the speedometer: we were doing eighty-five miles per hour, slaloming around the traffic. He steered with his left hand, his right arm casually thrown over the back of the passenger seat. I stared at his wrist hairs as I slid around in the back.

"Hey," he said, glancing back at me with a big grin. He wore aviator shades that completely hid his eyes; his mustache drooped past the corners of his mouth. "I bet you never thought you'd be riding in the backseat of a Tijuana cop car!"

"Not on purpose," I said.

It began innocently enough, with me babbling in abject terror.

I was geting my boots shined in one of those step-up shoeshine stalls you find all over Tijuana. It was like going to confession—the little booth had a wooden seat, and the only things visible to passersby were my feet. The gentleman buffing my left boot was wiry and bright with sweat. I settled in with a copy of *¡Alarma!*, Mexico's premier blood-drenched tabloid. As usual, it was full of satisfyingly lurid pictures: massacred cops, massacred drug dealers, car-wreck victims, cult murders, train-killed bodies.

We were on the corner of Ninth. A tan-clad arm flashed into the booth, its hard fist closing on my wrist. *A cop!* I jerked: *Oh my God! I'm busted!* For what, in retrospect, I don't know. I had wanted to meet a Tijuana cop, and had asked my relatives to arrange it, yet here I was blanching white and going utterly dry-mouthed. I had forgotten everything.

"What are you doing here, you son of a bitch," his voice snarled.

The shoeshine man, not knowing what was going on, backed away from my foot and sat on his haunches, watching. His face was completely blank.

"Ubb," I offered. "Ubba, ubba," I explained.

The cop's face peered in at me. I could see myself in his shades. He started to smile. Then he laughed. He asked me how I was doing. This apparently passed for humor among Tijuana's finest.

They are aware of their reputations. They cultivate their reputations. After all, nothing is more *macho* than causing immediate fear. They swagger, they beat people, they demand bribes, and they shoot. Members of my family have been officers of the Tijuana police force, yet I cut a wide swath around their brothers-in-arms, as does anyone with any sense.

Still, imagine being a cop in Tijuana. The mind reels. Here is a man called upon to preserve order in the most celebrated bastion of chaos on the border. This man is expected to enforce traffic laws in a country whose roads are haphazard at best, where stop signs often appear either twenty yards before an intersection—which is merely a dirt path straggling down to the road—or immediately after. There are no stop lines. No one minds the speed limits. And if he gives a *gringo* a traffic ticket, the *gringo* drives home and shows it to his friends and they have a good laugh and throw it away.

He works a city of famed vice: cascades of liquor, prostitution, child porn, drugs, even a healthy black market in fireworks and *faux* perfumes. His beat is visited by more *gringos* than visit Disneyland, and he has to judge which of these tourists are actually here to do harm, which are here to find innocent bargains, which have cocaine stuffed in their underwear, which carry knives, which are stoned or drunk or psychopathic.

His world is governed by laws that are effectively the reverse of ours: in Mexico, you are guilty until proven innocent. This leads to an enforced, endemic paranoia: of course you're lying—only a good lawyer will make anybody think otherwise. Add this policy to the already embattled and embittered mentality of a beat cop, and then stir in a Mexican loathing and resentment of *gringos*, and you're dealing with a difficult situation, at best. As a walking ambassador of American goodwill, you will invariably fail to impress.

And then, of course, there are the bribes. Mexicans call them *la mordida* (the bite). (American kids called cops "pigs" in the sixties, and Mexican kids called cops "dogs.") *La mordida* is not a private vice of the Mexican police. Anyone who has dealt with our friendly neighbor knows this. The phenomenon is too complex to dissect here—suffice it to say that it's a culture of patronage, with a long tradition of graft. It is a social Darwinist's dream, where the strong rule, and their strength is often measured by how much money they can extract from you for the most basic human need. It is a symbolic world where the money you pay out demonstrates your respect for the official and the official's position of merit, honor, and service.

In the case of the cops, add poverty.

Most police will tell you that no cop is paid enough. In Tijuana, as late as the early eighties, cops pulled in a whopping salary of twenty dollars a week. As if that weren't difficult enough, Tijuana cops buy their own guns. Motorcycle cops buy their own motorcycles. A handsome .357 Magnum with ivory grips and a Harley hog cost a bit more than any average officer can afford. Guess where they get their extra budgets.

I pulled myself from the shoeshine stand and was embarrassed that my knees shook. *Man,* I thought, *what a wimp.*

His shirt was open at the neck, showing black hair curling over the top of a brilliant white undershirt. The inevitable Dirty Harry Magnum rode high on his right hip. He wore knee boots polished bright as mirrors. Stripes ran up the sides of his tight pants.

"I just got a call I have to investigate. Want to come?"

"Yeah," I said.

"Let's go," he said, spinning on his heel and marching toward the police station.

We hopped into a cruiser, and he clicked on the radio, muttered his name, his destination, and a series of numbers.

"Hey, Pepe!" he called out the window. "I'm taking your car!"

"Fuck you!" Officer Pepe yelled back. Everybody laughed.

"Pinche Pepe," he said.

We wove down the street, impatiently honking at slow cars. Pedestrians on the corners gawked at me in the back with the same slack-faced look of dread I suddenly realized I had on my face every time a prisoner was whisked past me in the back of one of those cars.

"Look at this," the cop was saying. Cars refused to allow him through the intersection. "Nobody gives a damn about the law!"

He hit his siren, gestured, waved his arms.

"¡*Policía!*" he snapped out the window. "Get out of the way!"

Tijuana's downtown gridlock suddenly broke and we shot through.

"Nobody loves a cop," he said.

"Don't say I said so," he said, "but there are a lot of crooked officers on this force."

"Really?" I said, trying to sound bland.

He shrugged, raised both hands. The car steered itself for twenty feet. "That's life. What did you expect? This is Tijuana."

We came upon a gap in the center island.

"Hold on," he said.

Before I knew what we were doing, he threw us into a power slide, sideways through the gap. The car fishtailed in front of oncoming traffic, then the tires bit into the road and we shot off in the opposite direction, still going a respectable seventy-five.

"Not bad, eh?" he said.

"Wow," I said.

"I'll show *you* who can drive," he said.

"No! Please!" I cried. I thought twice about making any jokes about police cruelty or torture of suspects. Instead, I said, "Tell me more about corruption."

"A few years ago," he said, "we were getting a lot of hassle from the San Diego police. We had car thieves working on our force. San Diego told us, 'Look. You can't do this. You can't steal American cars. You're cops!' "

He glanced back at me. "Lots of these *cabrones* have new Toyota pickups. Where do you think they got them?"

We slowed abruptly and left the main road, cutting up a hill at the north end of Tijuana. We passed under a narrow railroad bridge and hit rough patches of dirt.

"Those crooked cops," he said, "make it hard for us who want to be honest. Some of us are good cops. But now all of us get investigated all the time."

We were heading up into Colonia Libertad, the notorious *barrio* where illegals and *coyotes* gathered every night to go into the canyons. Lawlessness had enjoyed a vogue in those hills for so long that police didn't care to venture there at night. My guide said, "Watch out up here. These people are animals. They don't give a shit about anything. If they catch us in a dead end, they'll hit us with rocks. Stay with me and keep your mouth shut."

"Yes, sir," I said.

Apparently, a bus had run over a guy on a motorcycle. Someone called it in to police headquarters, but nobody knew how long ago. When we got there, the twisted bike was lying in the dirt. It was a small Japanese machine. The bus had backed out of a blind drive, climbed over the bike and the rider, and continued backing out.

"You didn't see him?" demanded the cop.

"No," said the driver.

"You didn't *feel* him?"

"No."

The cop rubbed his face, looked around. "Where's the cyclist?"

Everybody shrugged.

"Is he dead?"

Shrugs. "Maybe." "No." "I don't know."

Mud around the crushed bike could have been blood. Then again, it could have been oil or gas or urine.

"Did an ambulance take him?"

"No," said the bus driver. Then, "A car. One of the neighbors."

Clearly angry by now, the cop took his name and address. "We'll be coming for you," he said ominously.

The driver's eyebrows shot up in alarm, but before the cop could be reasoned with, he was back in his car. On the hill, *cholos* yelled slang insults at him: "Hey *chota*" (a nickname for "cop"), *"fuck you!"*

Grimly, he backed out and floored it, pelting the crowd with gravel. They skipped and danced in his cloud of dust.

"We're going to the city hospital," he said. "It's a butcher shop. Don't say anything when we get there, because they don't like people seeing their emergency rooms. I'll tell them you're a detective."

We arrived on the emergency ramp in a burst of lights.

"Walk fast," he said, hitching up his gunbelt.

I followed him at my best police-inspector clip. We stormed through the doors, brushing past a concerned orderly who wanted us to halt. On our way into the bowels of the hospital, however, we were accosted by an old nurse. She held up her hand and commanded us to stop. "What is your business?" she asked.

"Investigating an accident," the cop said.

"And this gentleman?"

"Detective."

I looked too much like a *gringo*.

"Sí, señora," I said in my best Spanish.

Like a relentless gnome in a Monty Python skit, she badgered us. "Does he have ID?" she demanded of the cop.

"Ma'am," he said, exasperated, "he's *undercover!*"

This arcane police word seemed to work on her, and she relented.

"Follow me," she said.

Although there were surely no flies in the hospital, they remain my overwhelming impression of the place. I imagine big-assed flies bumping into everything. Dust and dirt formed small wedges in the corners, dirty bandages were visible on the floors of rooms standing empty, middle-aged women lay on stretchers in the hall obviously suffering from something that was not readily visible. We glanced into the various emergency cubicles as we went down the hall. Innumerable fascinating scenes were enacted in each, but no biker. The last stall featured the nightmarish vision of a nurse leaning over a boy's face with pliers of some sort. She had latched on to something and was trying to work it out. He writhed and shouted, flat on his back, arms and legs strapped down. She paused in her efforts and looked up at us, plier handles still firmly in her grip. The cop blandly stared at this tableau, then looked at me and wiggled his eyebrows up and down. "Interesting," he said.

Outside, he said, "Well, who knows where the motorcyclist is." We got in the car. "Fuck him. Let's go."

So we went back to the station.

I entered with some dread.

"Keep out of the way," he said, going in to make out his report.

A small group of Americans was seated on a bench. One of the women had slivers of glass in her face; she was dabbing at the blood with tissues. Various cops milled around the bench looking down at the kids. The official *policía* translator hovered over them. He was a smarmy disco-king in a shiny silken shirt and slicked-back hair.

"Hello, frien'," he said to them. "Hello, baby."

"Please," the cut woman said.

"Baby," the translator said, "you go to jail." It sounded as though he were asking her if she attended Yale.

"Everybody," he said, gesturing at the lot of them, "going to Yale!"

He beamed, as though they had just won a raffle.

"They have to be investigated," the cop said behind me. He must have filed a short report.

"But they're hurt," I said.

"That's what happens in a car wreck, *amigo.*"

Too dazed to be terrified, the *gringo* kids slumped on the seat looking stringy and tattered.

"She needs help," I said.

The cop pursed his lips. He took a better look, apparently suspicious that she was faking the glass in her face.

"Hmm," he said.

"Don't worry, frien'," said the translator. "No problem!"

I didn't dare speak to the kids. I had no idea what codes of behavior and protocol I might be breaking. I certainly didn't want to join them in Yale.

The cop went to talk to the captain, who stepped out of his office and scowled at me, then at them. This was obviously highly irregular.

"Martínez!" he snapped at some distant officer. "Get this girl some medical attention."

He vanished back into his office.

All the cops seemed shocked by this development. They

stood there staring at the kids on the bench. One of them finally detached himself from the mob and tenderly took the young woman by the arm and pulled her up. Then he looked around, wondering what to do with her. They turned and disappeared into the interior of the station, and the translator was cooing, "Okay, baby. Is o-kay."

Dark was falling. He was going off-duty.

"I'll give you a ride to where you're going," he said. We wandered back over to Pepe's car and got in again.

"You can sit in the front," he said.

He took off his shades, worked his crackling neck, rubbed his eyes.

"What a job," he said.

We backed out, cruised slowly. His eyes compulsively scanned the sidewalks, flicked from door to door, lit fleetingly on faces as we passed.

"A Salvadoran got his tongue cut out over here," he said, pointing to a corner. "How do you like that? Right down the street from the police station. *Pinche* gang of *cholos* get hold of this poor guy and cut out his tongue. What do you do with people like that?"

Next block.

"This old man came up to me this morning. Some crazy *pendejo* killed his dog over there." He pointed. "He pulled the dog out of the old man's truck and kicked it to death."

He shook his head. "What are you going to do," he said.

It was fully dark by now.

"That's a great disco, over there," he said. "You should try it." Marko's Jet-Set Disco.

"You have a strange job," I said.

He smiled.

"It's not so bad," he said. "Hey! You know my favorite thing about being a cop?" He pulled over and stopped, turned around in the seat to face me. Tijuana's one last honest cop.

"What?" I said.

"Disco patrol."

"Disco patrol?"

"Yeah. It starts at two or three in the morning. We hang around on the side streets, watching for American women driving alone." He was really smiling now. "These dumb broads come down here by themselves to dance and pick up Mexicans."

"Oh, really," I said.

"So they come out of the discos and head for the border, and if they're alone, or there's two of them, I pull them over."

"Ticket," I said.

"Exactly. I turn on my lights, hit the siren—it scares them. They pull over. I get out of the car, mad as hell. I tell them they ran a red light."

"And you charge them a bribe?" I offered.

"A *bribe!*" he barked. "Don't make me laugh. I tell them they have to go to jail. I arrest them. Then I get them in the car. Then I pull out my lariat." *(La reata.)* He pantomimed laying a penis clearly nineteen inches long across the steering wheel.

"I tell them, 'Suck on this and you can go.' And you know what? *Gringas* are sluts—they always suck my lariat."

"Oh," I said.

He drove me to my destination in silence.

When we got there, I said, "Do you let them go?"

He said, "Of course I let them go! I'm a cop, not a monster."

CHAPTER EIGHT

The Last Soldier
of Pancho Villa

Leaving Tijuana by way of the free road to Ensenada takes you through a dusty poverty that is suggestive of ancient days. The canyons bristle with shacks and tumbled fences, while above, *maquiladoras* (foreign-owned factories) crown the hills in castlelike sprawls. The serfs below await the day the complexes above them will open their doors. The hillsides seem to crumble as you watch them. Yards are dust. On the slopes, where the soil is often shades of gray, the people have built ingenious gardens using abandoned car tires. They dig the tires into the slope, then fill them with dirt. Often, whole hillsides will be made of a staggered, sloping wall of tires. In each tire, a plant or two— geraniums and *nopales* (beavertail cactus) are most common. (You can eat *nopales*, and since geraniums grow from cuttings, certain *barrio* folk launch garden after garden for their neighbors.)

Then, the *yonkes*. Abandoned discos. *Yonkes*. A Catholic orphanage. *Yonkes*. The infantry base. Then you come around a bend into fields of flowers—buttercups and mustard splash yellow over the hills. It's surprising. If you're not prepared, it might startle you to pop out of the sprawl of the city so suddenly. The sea seems to rise in the distance. The cars spread out on the road and begin to speed, clean wind tearing in through the windows.

There are small towns before and beyond Rosarito. Near one of them, there is a rock in the ocean that has the same shape as a Volkswagen beetle. It looks like it's driving to Hawaii. You will see a bright red building on the right. This is the orphanage that has always been run by Mama and Papa T.

Mama had no teeth. Her nose was a mass of brown scars from years of continuous sunburn. She was always either forty-

nine or seventy, there was no way to tell. You heard her before
you saw her. She was either laughing, scolding a child or a dog,
or crying out in her joy that you came to see her. *"¡Oh! ¡Oh!"*
she'd shout. *"¡Qué bueno!"*

She plowed into your ribs as you got out of your vehicle. If
you seemed at all friendly, she gave you a fierce hug. She patted
you on the arms, back, sides, chest, in the manner of poor old
Mexican women—her palm open, her fingers stiff enough so
they bent back a little. Her touch was so light you hardly felt it.
It was almost as though she were touching you to let herself
know you were really there.

Then she was apt to hold her open hand up by your face—it
looked as though you might get slapped—and offer an ecstatic
soliloquy that clearly included God, missionaries, and abundant
blessings. You might even have gotten a tour of the compound.
Mama was proud of her new American toilets and bathtubs. If
you took her doughnuts, you could expect to end up in her
kitchen, watching her sop up coffee and slurp them down.

Papa, however, was more reserved. He was a shadow. You
would see him in the background, his slightly palsied head
nodding gently in a white hardhat.

Papa, unlike Mama, was ninety. In 1978, he was ninety, and
in 1991, he seemed to still be ninety. His skin was dark brown,
brown as mahogany. His mustache was white and sparse, small
enough to look like a trace of milk he forgot to lick off his lip.
His brown eyes were so faded, so encircled by cataracts and
clouded with years, that they looked almost blue. He was five
feet tall.

In his youth, Papa rode a horse. He carried a rifle. He rode
hard into desert towns and saw army garrisons fall. He slept on

the ground, wrapped in a thin blanket. You might see him in some of those old Mexican photographs, with gunbelts crossed over his heart. Long before he became a Christian, Papa T. was a soldier of Pancho Villa. And when any commotion happened at his orphanage, Papa retreated into his own silence. He hid in the big chicken coop under the water tower. If you followed him, you saw a pale shape standing in there. He held the chickens to his lips. He had a few favorites. He fancied some fluffy white show chickens someone gave him. "Feel this," he'd say. You'd pet the chicken. Its feathers felt like cat fur. "Soft," he'd say, his delighted laughter quiet, his voice a reed in wind. "Soft!" He'd kiss the chicken on the head.

Papa built the orphanage by hand. He first made it of wood, hauling lumber from Tijuana, Rosarito, even Ensenada. At the time, the people of the small fishing village were curious if not suspicious. Papa made a long two-story building, with his and Mama's dwelling at the west end. Boys would live downstairs, and girls above. Papa called the place the "Home of Light." (*Hogar de Luz.*) When he finished building, he painted it sky blue.

Then, as a service to the children and the community, he built a church next door. He and his sons labored for almost a year, using cement, stucco, and wood. It was the first Protestant church on that part of the coast. Once the church was done, Papa realized the orphanage needed modernizing, so he hauled out his ladders and hammers again and began an ambitious construction project behind the original orphanage. This one would be entirely of brick and cement block, with modern bathrooms and dorm rooms throughout. American work crews eagerly joined in, bringing him supplies and fresh-faced youth groups who scrambled up and down Papa's ladders, slopping cement and banging nails.

On those days, Papa stood watching, his ever-present white helmet bobbing slightly. He gripped either a huge white cup of coffee or a banana. He pointed sometimes, then looked at me, as if some secret between us had just been confirmed.

At the end of the day, he thanked everybody. As soon as they were on the highway back north, he climbed his ladder and undid the work they had done wrong. Often, Papa spent two days fixing angles and rehammering frames.

"It's all right," he said. "The young people need to work. It's good for them to have work."

Because of his age, and his bobbing head, Americans made the mistake of thinking him simple, or diminished in some way. Once, a missionary crew descended on him to repaint his orphanage. They had brought bright red paint, so the orphanage would be easier to spot. Papa liked it blue. The Americanos forged ahead, and the leader of the crew said to me, "Tell him he's a good man." Then he patted Papa on the head.

Papa stood there, shoulders hunched, shaking a little.

He then offered me the only unsolicited comment I ever heard him make about Pancho Villa. "At least Pancho Villa," he said, "was a gentleman. He let a man have self-respect."

Things went on as normal in the newly red orphanage until one day we pulled into the driveway and found Mama crying and wringing her hands. We thought Papa had died. She held on to us and wailed.

Papa had left home.

Papa had this recurring dream. If you were friends with him, he'd tell it to you. "Jesus Christ is calling me," he'd say. He heard Jesus almost every night, with the clarity of the dreams of old men. No matter what he did, Jesus intruded on his dreams, took him from whatever reverie he was in and led him back to the same insistent vision.

He saw a vast, barren plain. It was stark, dead. Nothing grew there. The sun was white. He could hear the empty sound of wind. Jesus would stride toward him. In His hand, a seed. He pressed the seed into Papa's hand and indicated he was to plant it where they stood. "Here my tree will grow," Jesus said. "Here you will build my house."

Papa cried sometimes, talking about it. He thought he was supposed to die there. He was afraid to go into the desert, fueled by nothing more than a dream. But he was a soldier, and he'd been in the desert before. He had his orders. He put it off as long as he could—he put it off until he knew his life was over. If he was to die out there, at least he had done his work for the children. He told Mama good-bye one morning, took a small bag of things and a blanket, and walked up to the highway. The children cried; Mama wrung her hands and pleaded. The last they saw of him was the white helmet through the window of a bus.

We were reduced to the religious platitudes you offer people of faith: "You'll see him again in heaven."

"Yes!" she cried. "Glory be to God!"

Two months passed. A stranger appeared at the Home of Light, asking for Mama. Was she related to a Sr. T?

"Yes!" she cried. "Oh yes!" Tears ran down her cheeks.

Did Sr. T wear a helmet, and was he . . . elderly?

"Yes!"

The man sipped a cup of coffee at Mama's table. He related a story of what he had seen in the great northern desert of Mexico. An old man got off a bus in a desert hamlet where this man had a small business. The locals watched him hobble along with his bedroll and bag. He approached an Indian man. He was a Yaqui. They watched this stranger talk to the Yaqui man for a few minutes, then the two of them turned and hiked out of town together.

Later, when the Yaqui man came into town for supplies, he reported that the old man had brought him a message from Jesus. They were busy building a new house for God out on the plain. The townsfolk regularly visited the site. Papa somehow accumulated tools, supplies, and helpers.

"Tell Mama," he told the visitor, "that the Indians are building a church. It is going well."

This fellow had business in Tijuana, and was so curious about this marvelous scene that he promised to drive down the coast and report to Mama.

After the end of the summer, we drove into the compound. Halloween was approaching soon, and the searing heat of late September had finally drifted off as though it had never happened. Mama wore a bright dress, a scarf tied over her hair. She danced around, clapping her hands like a kid.

"He's back!" she shouted. "He's back! He's back!"

We thought she meant one of us until we realized it was Papa.

"Where is he?" I said.

"With the chickens."

I went down to the chicken house. It was dark in there. I pulled open the wire door and stepped through. The floor was three inches of chicken dung.

"Papa?" I said. "Are you in here?"

A small blob of white stirred down at the end. That famous helmet.

I went in deeper.

"Papa!" I said.

He had a white chicken in his hands. He held it out to me. He gestured at me with the chicken.

"Feel these feathers," he said.

I petted the chicken.

Papa glanced at me.

Looking somewhat amused, he leaned over and confided a secret.

"I lived," he said.

CHAPTER NINE

Meet the Satánicos

Christmas was coming. Up north, the *gringos* had just celebrated their Thanksgiving. Tijuana, as always, was beginning to
copy them, and many families here, too, had enjoyed "El Tenks-
geevee." In Spanish, it is *el día de las gracias,* though what
exactly Mexicans have to give thanks for on North America's
Thanksgiving is not clear. Perhaps they're thanking God the
Pilgrims landed in Massachusetts.

In *barrios* and *colonias,* orphanages and garbage dumps,
hope stirred as the cold descended. In spite of the illness and
the discomfort of late fall, they knew that the missionaries were
preparing Christmas for them. Orphanages picked reluctant
children to wrap themselves in sheets and blankets to play
Mary, Joseph, and the Wise Men in their yearly pageants. Invariably, a doll that had lost 75 percent of its hair played Jesus.
And there always seemed to be a boy who had to crawl around
on all fours playing the ass. The orphanage directors opened
their doors to neighbors—thinking, somehow, that these Christmas plays would evangelize all the *barrio,* causing a mass exo-
dus from Catholicism, a spiritual flocking to the Protestant banner.

The *colonia* was one of the new ones that caused so much
controversy in Tijuana. It will remain nameless here. This was
its first Christmas with Von and his crew. Created unofficially
by *paracaidistas,* or "parachutists," the clever Mexican nickname for squatters who descend on a piece of land from out of
nowhere, it lay two hills over from the old dump area, and it was
rumored to be under the control of a gangster who involved
entire *barrios* in car thievery. Driving in, I was struck immediately by the rows of automotive husks lining the rough dirt

street; in some places, stripped and burned-out cars were layered on top of each other. Certain arroyos were clogged with car bodies, many of them on their roofs. Yet this colorful so-called gangster took an interest in the missionaries of the area, and he looked out for their well-being. Often his largesse had to be politely deflected—one drug-treatment program in the area graciously rejected his repeated offers of new cars.

The *colonia*, being controversial, indeed not officially in existence, lacked any services whatsoever. Aside from the typical lack of water, there was no electricity. There was no bus service. There were no telephones, no streetlights, no doctor's offices, stores, schools. And there was certainly no police presence. The *barrio* was the Wild West. The missionary from the treatment center told me of his Saturday nights—he and the addicts in their plywood church and dorms, looking into the pitch-black canyons below them, watched the gunfire flash, listened to the yells and shouting. "Everything happens here on Saturday nights," he said. "Anything you can imagine. *Anything.*"

The vans rattled up the hill, cut left into a small clear area at the crest. Beyond lay the deep black of the unsettled outskirts. The missionaries built a lit basketball court and a small clubhouse for the *barrio* kids. A gasoline generator made a racket. Kids flocked to the ball court and the clubhouse all through the fall. They had nothing else to do on the hill except sleep, listen to radios, or sniff glue. None of them could afford drugs, and few of them could afford booze.

The local criminal element was a street gang called Los Satánicos. They gathered along the edge of the ball court, arrayed themselves along the retaining wall that kept the top of the hill from burying the youth center. They'd been sniffing glue and paint thinner.

Inside, foosball tables, video games. Scruffy children in various shades of adobe-brown competed noisily. Pastor Von provided them with about six elaborate ray guns, and they used them to shoot at flashing electrical targets. In a corner, a terrified head-banger in a Metallica T-shirt squatted on his haunches. His brown face was blotchy with panic, going an ugly ash-gray. Various *vatos* and *cholos* gathered around him. He had made the terminal mistake of punching the little brother of one of the Satánicos. They cornered him in the building. At one point, they sent in an expedition that clubbed him over the head with a hunk of cement. Efren, a *veterano* of these streets and one of Von's full-time employees, chased them out. "This is a Christian place," he told them. "Fight outside, not in here."

When spoken to, the head-banger did not respond. Once he got over the shock of the head blow, he stood up and assumed an air of nonchalance, pushing some smaller boys out of the way at the foosball table. His eyes darted to the door regularly; he was trapped and he knew it. Spies from the Satánicos filtered out the door to report on his condition.

Some of the recovering addicts from the treatment center watched the gang nervously. They had a strangely somber mien, quiet men with mournful eyes. "This is no good," one of them told me. "This situation is very bad. They're going to get him."

The Satánicos waited along the edge of the ball court. One boy sat on the retaining wall; a bearded boy was lying back between his legs. The top boy wrapped his legs around the bottom boy's abdomen and pulled him close. He rested his chin tenderly on his head, slipped his hands across his chest and belly. One of them had brought a pit bull. Another had a small black canister of Mace he compulsively pulled in and out of his pocket. They murmured their plans, laughing. The only girls hid at the far end of the gang—two thirteen- or fourteen-year-olds, with hard-sprayed *chola* hairdos rising in black splashes off their heads. A Satánico in a dusty black trench coat pulled a six-inch-long switchblade from his pocket, flicked it open. They laughed. He cut the air. "How do you like it?" he said to his invisible victim. He stabbed. "Are you still alive?" he said. The Satánicos were excited. The ballplayers on the court ignored them: a drive to the basket, a hard shoulder block, a lay-up that clattered through the rim. The pit bull sat somberly, watching.

"They're going to cut him up," the addict told me. "They're going to make shredded meat—*machaca.*"

Nobody could figure out how to get the Metallica boy out of the building. Perhaps, one of the missionaries suggested, we could divert the attention of the Satánicos for a minute, and the boy could jump out the back window.

Von said, "He's trapped in the building, eh?"

We nodded.

"Well," he said, "at least he'll be sure to stick around for the Bible study."

Then a curious thing happened. Four big old-timers, maybe nineteen or twenty years old, wandered into the alley outside the clubhouse. They all wore billed caps, and had long hair. Two of them had nut-brown scars on their faces, and their shoulders rocked as they walked. The Satánicos stowed the knife immediately, and they shuffled nervously. The four *veteranos* swaggered into the clubhouse and scanned the kids within. They gestured at the Metallica boy: come.

One of the addicts pulled me aside.

"They're his brothers," he said.

"An escort!"

"Yes. The Satánicos are bad, but these ones are *bad*. They came here to kill, not fight."

They appeared at the door of the clubhouse. They formed a rough diamond around the head-banger, a flying wedge. He grew cocky in their embrace, heavy-lidded and inscrutable. The Satánicos looked at their feet. One innocently busied himself with his pit bull.

The *veteranos* strolled along the top of the wall where the Satánicos sat; they walked up the slope, all four of them staring steadily at the gang, offering them a silent challenge. Nobody took them up on it. Nobody even looked. Eye contact would mean disaster. The only sound on the hill was the squeaking tennis shoes of the ballplayers rushing the net, the laughter of the children inside. The lead *veterano* snorted in derision, and the group vanished into the dark.

The Satánicos were suddenly revealed, in the pale light of the ball court, to be boys and girls, confused and chastened. The one with the knife was a skinny little geek with big ears and sticks for legs. The girls faded away, perhaps avoiding the Satánicos' wrath. The one boy holding the other nuzzled his ear, clutched him tight from behind. The one with the Mace suddenly scuttled along the edge of the court, threatening to Mace one of the players, but even this threat collapsed. These children were not helpless—they held up missionaries at gunpoint out in the street—but that night, their ferocity collapsed on them, just for an instant, and they seemed lost, unable to get it back.

The pit bull, all soulful eyes, nuzzled my knee.
"He's vicious," one of the Satánicos warned me.
"A fighter," I offered.
"Vicious. A killer."
I bent down to the dog. He put out his paw to shake hands.

CHAPTER TEN

Father's Day

(Thanks to my brother, Juan Francisco Urrea, for providing information that would have otherwise been unavailable to me.)

January 10. My father, in a red American Motors 440, drives north through the Sonora desert, ticking off towns as the sun rises to his right: Santa Ana, Caborca, Tajito. He is on his way to Tijuana, to his mother's house, where he has lived on and off since my mother threw him out of our home. He left Culiacán yesterday, in the morning. He's been driving alone, nonstop, pausing for gas and two terrible roadside meals. The cheap tape recorder nestled among packs of cigarettes on the seat beside him has been playing Mexican songs that call forth all his ghosts and memories. Miguel Prado, Agustín Lara, Pedro Infante, Lola Beltrán. Mile upon mile, the car has gradually filled with the dead and forgotten. The backseat is crowded with a hundred girlfriends, lovers, and wives. Time swirls around him like smoke. His dentures fit badly—the pain keeps him awake. He has spent Christmas in his hometown, in the farthest southern corner of Sinaloa, and he has recognized no one. All of them are old and strange to him. Their concerns are foolish, their laughter painful to his ears. He has retrieved a thousand dollars from the bank on Morelos Street, a gift for me. My father is sixty-one years old.

San Luis Río Colorado appears in the shimmering early light. He is driving fast—he always drove fast. Far away, Yuma, Arizona, suggests itself through the haze. The Mexican checkpoint is outside of town. Bored and aggressive Mexican Immigration and Federal Judicial Police officers wave cars over and inspect papers. They deny passage randomly, confiscate valuable-looking goods, exact "tolls" from *gringos* and border Mexicans who lack the papers or the conviction to convince the officers they may proceed. My father is Mexican, but he is also blond and blue-eyed. (His blond hair has gone white, but his skin is still pale pink, and his eyes behind his glasses are still bright.) He has California plates on his car. He is going fast.

This is where the thing happens.

No one knows exactly what, or if it happened before the *aduana* (customs inspection) huts or after. But somehow, my father—Mexican ballads rattling through the cheap speakers, all those voices in his head, smoking a cigarette, smoke trailing from his mouth like he's burning already and going down—leaves the road and sails into the desert dawn.

His car sails for a dreadful instant, forever. Angles off the road and lifts into the air. Unimaginable movement of fists on the wheel, trying to right the car after it has taken flight. Dust and gravel cresting beneath him like a wave, as he catapults over the edge of a drop-off. Everything in the car—tapes, cigarettes, ashes, coins, recorder, my father's glasses—comes to life and eddies around him. The car tips. Its front corner digs into the ground. It flips once, twice. Later, rumors suggest it rolled six times. The wheel breaks off in his hands. The windshield vanishes. He goes out the window. The car rolls on him. He is dragged back in by the lurching force of the crash. All around, his things scatter across the sand and sage.

It is easy to imagine the silence returning then. Increments of peace. The wind can be heard again, then the calling of crows and jays. In the distance, a siren.

I am not brought into this story until late.

Without me, my father goes about the business of dying. He tries not to die, of course. My father would not surrender easily to death. But the Mexicans manage to convince him.

Before they take him to the hospital, various agents of the Mexican Republic help themselves to the sudden flea market my father has set out for them. As he bleeds on the gurney, blind and mute, pissing his pants, they sift through the goods: there are a lot of tapes, after all. Someone nabs his recorder. Someone else takes a fancy to his new shoes, bought for him by my favorite cousin and given to him only two days before.

His wallet and my thousand dollars are safe—soaked in urine in his pockets. Nobody cares to fish for them at the moment. Because nobody wants to reach into all that mess, they don't find out he's a Mexican citizen, a retired army officer, late of the presidential staff of Mexico, and a retired federal cop. He can't talk to tell them. They drive off, blue lights inconsequential against the sun.

In town, they strip him naked and call in a Mexican doctor.

The doctor says something along the lines of "My God, it's Beto!"

One of the attendants says something else, like "What do you mean, *Beto?*"

The doctor looks around him. He can't believe it. This is too strange. Just days ago, he was at a party with my father in Sinaloa. He'd asked my father for a ride to this very town. My father turned him down, saying, cryptically, "I don't want to be responsible for your life."

"I know this man," the doctor says. "He's a Mexican."

Somebody calls the police. The *Federales* are on their way. Something strange is going on here, and the doctor wants nothing to do with it. He snaps some orders to the staff of the clinic, then plunges his hand into my father's pockets. He is no doubt startled to find a thousand dollars there, in new bills. He takes my father's wallet out of the back pocket and flees. For reasons that will remain unclear, the *Federales* will spend the rest of the day trying to find him to get all these things back from him. He will be so busy avoiding them that he will not see my father again.

Once the doctor leaves, they wheel my father, naked, into a room. He is beginning to struggle, to writhe around in his bed. His ribs are cracked; his internal injuries bleed within him; his chin is split, and he might have a concussion; he has some brain injuries and might have suffered a stroke. Nobody's quite sure what's wrong with him. They decide to quiet him down and shoot him with morphine.

My father, drugged, settles back into a velvet haze. All his ghosts swarm to him and begin to smother him.

I have siblings whom I know and don't know: Juan, Alberto, Octavio, Leticia, and Martha. The circumstances of my father's life took him from them at an early age, and they were left to struggle with their mother. I am younger than all of them, and have never lived with any of them. Like me, they fear him and worship him and miss him even when he's with us. Somehow, word gets out on the border that Alberto Urrea has been seriously hurt in a car wreck. But people think it's my brother Alberto. People start looking for my brother's family to tell them he's dying.

In the meantime, in our old neighborhood in Tijuana, my aunt Lety and cousin Hugo are in the family house on Rampa Independencia. They are waiting for Beto to arrive from Sinaloa. Hugo has built him a small bedroom where he keeps all his tokens—love letters, bowling trophies, moldering *Playboy* magazines, a box of photographs. In those photos, my father is a skinny boy with a heart-shaped mouth. He looks sad in every one. The years have tinted them all brown.

My aunt hears my father's car idling in front of the house. She glances out and sees a red shape pull up to her gate.

"It's Beto!" she calls. My grandmother, gone mad with age, blinks in her chair like a pudgy bird.

"Who?" she says.

"Beto," says my aunt. *Beto ya llego.* " (Beto has arrived.)

She steps outside to greet him. There is no car there. She steps into the street. Looks both ways. No red car in sight.

"Beto's dead," she says.

Word spreads—the doctor calls my aunt. Somehow, she and Alberto make contact, and they, along with my cousin Hugo and my father's former wife, Emilia, head east in Alberto's car. Strangely enough, it is a vast black Cadillac: they rush to my father's death in a hearse.

Other relatives go into a Mexican version of action: one branch grabs the first plane they can that flies to Arizona. In their panic, they don't realize the ticketing agent has sent them to the wrong part of Arizona. The flight leaves them farther from my father than if they'd stayed in Tijuana.

Somebody finally calls me in San Diego. I have been listening to music—something as ridiculous as Uriah Heep. Everyone has left for San Luis Río Colorado. Everything is happening. I am asked to hold steady. Someone will get right back to me. Nobody does.

My cousin Hugo, the most feared member of the family, is the one who finally tells me what it was like to find my father in the clinic. Hugo was raised by him, and knows him better than some of his own sons. Hugo calls him "Papá."

Family legend has it that once, when Hugo was driving

through Tijuana late at night, a carload of *cholos* began to harass him, trying to push him off the road, yelling taunts. Hugo calmly pulled over, took a homemade broadsword out from under the seat, and proceeded to chop pieces off their car. He split their hood with it, pulled it out, and said, "All right, come on."

They abandoned their car and ran into the night.

Hugo pushes his way into the room and sits on the bed, holds my writhing father down. Tells him, "Don't worry, Papa. We're here. We'll get you out."

My father cannot say anything to him, but Hugo senses he understands. He calms down, lies back. Hugo talks to him for a moment more.

According to what faction of the Urrea family you consult, either of the following occurs:

Arrangements are made to transport my father to the border, and there, an American ambulance will carry him into Yuma. Hugo knows my father will die if left in this clinic. The American ambulance arrives at the border crossing and waits, off to the side, doors open, light circling.

No Mexican unit arrives. Repeated calls reveal nothing: nobody knows what happened to the ambulance. Isn't it there? It ought to be there. How curious.

It never arrives. Hugo and my father wait for an hour. It has been eight hours since the accident.

Or:

Hugo and my aunt Lety and my brother Alberto and his mother, Emilia, gather and make the evacuation plans. But my aunt, seeing too clearly what is about to happen, convinces them to abandon hope. *Beto is going to die*, she tells them. *Can't you see?*

Finally, the ghosts convince my father. He settles back in the bed, eyes looking at nothing in particular. Without a word or a gesture, my father dies.

A few miles away, the Americans close their doors, turn off their lights, and drive back to Yuma.

Too late to do any good, I enter the picture.

Hugo's sister, Margo, picks me up on her way to Tijuana. A family friend has called me and told me the news. Margo's car is crammed with silent people as we ride into Tijuana and rise up to Independencia, shoulders digging into each other as the car hits the ruts and half-buried boulders in the road.

We gather in the dirt street outside the family home: Hugo, Aunt Lety, Margo, the riders, me. Dogs behind the fence think we're having a party. They think the fun's about to begin. They dance on their back legs, eagerly watching us in the street.

"Let's go," Hugo says. He means to the funeral home: Funeraria González.

I get in Hugo's truck. Hugo has been the closest to the thing. He has accumulated a kind of evil grace. I hope he can tell me if anything special happened. If there were any apparitions, sounds, lights, angels.

"He died," he says. For him, that's enough.

We drive downtown. The funeral home is nondescript, in the middle of a run-down block. But then, most blocks in Tijuana are run-down, all cobbled together with no plan in mind, facade after mid-fifties facade leaning into each other, paint coming away from the walls on thin wedges of stucco.

The brothers are waiting for me outside. We don't want to take a step without each other. Nobody knows how to grieve. We stand apart from each other with a strange military precision, two feet between each man. We shuffle. We grin: the old man's dead. We shake our heads, sigh. We laugh. Nobody can fit the fact into the day. They have my father's money and wallet. The doctor has turned them over to somebody, I don't know who, and it has appeared here, in front of the funeral home. My eldest brother, Juan, hands me the cash. It's floppy. Wet, it feels like felt.

"It must have rained," somebody says. "Do you think it rained? Everything's all wet."

Hugo looks at me. He says nothing. I know why it's wet. Hugo and Juan know why it's wet. Juan and I stare into each other's eyes.

I say, "I guess they had an early-morning shower."

Everybody nods.

Juan gives me the wallet. Inside: driver's license, green card, social security card, notes, slips of paper, useless cards in various shades of blue and yellow. In his picture, my father looks small and old. He has a pouch under his chin. You can see the curve of his skull under the diminishing front rank of his hair.

"Okay," I say.

We turn as one and enter the door.

Hugo grabs my arm as the brothers start upstairs. "Down here," he says.

"What," I say.

"The body's down here," he says.

"So?"

"So you're going to look at it."

"No I'm not."

"Yes you are. You're going to look at it."

"No."

Hugo has a habit of always speaking English to me. For some reason, I insist on speaking Spanish to him. I'm not sure what it is we're trying to convince each other of.

"It's up to you," he says. "He's all banged up. You've got to decide if it's an open casket or not. That's what he'd want. Come on."

His grip is bony as a talon as he pulls me into the little room. The casket is on a stone bench, about three feet off the ground. Mexican floral arrangements have begun to surround the coffin: horseshoes on stands, wreaths, all of them draped in *faux*-satin sashes with family names and condolences written across them in glue and glitter. They look like entrants in a retirement-home flower-arranging contest, or good luck displays at a high school reunion.

Hugo uses his pocketknife to unscrew the lid. The screw rises, rises, interminably coming up until it wiggles loose and he says, "Look," and I put my hands on the lid and wait. "Go on," he says. I resent his manliness more than anything on earth at that instant, then I lift the lid. For some reason, I hold my breath, like my father is going to smell. But he's encased in glass. In fact, he probably does smell—he's been dead now for two days with no embalming. Many Mexican funeral homes just clamp a sheet of glass over the body to prevent any problems, and you look down at them as though you were in a glass-bottomed boat, drifting across the shoals of Hell. It's alarming. You think, *He can't breathe in there.*

I look in. He's small as a ten-year-old boy in a faded brown photograph. He's unimaginably sad, his lips turned a little around his injured mouth, looking as though he's about to say a word that begins with *m.* I stare down at my father, my only father, and my breath fogs the glass and steals his face.

Open wounds turn black after death.

"Close it," I say.

Hugo shuts the lid gently.

"Don't screw it down," I say. "He wouldn't want people to see him like that, but I think they have a right to say good-bye, if they want to. So they can lift the lid for themselves."

It is my first decision as a grown man.

"Good," Hugo says. "That's the right choice."

Upstairs, my brother Juan is waiting for me. The others stand behind him.

"There's a problem," he says.

"What problem?"

"We owe some money," he says, "for the body."

"We what?"

A pleasant short man steps up. He has a tan police uniform, but no badge or gun. He's a lackey for the San Luis Río Colorado cops.

"I brought the body," he says.

"Thank you," I tell him.

"They said to tell you," he glances away, "that the body is still in custody."

We all look at each other, eyes clicking in steady sweeps of all the faces.

"You're kidding," I say.

"No, señor," he says. "The police department still has possession of your father. I have been instructed to ask you for the fee to release him to you."

"You want me to pay bail for a corpse?"

The man is uncomfortable. He says nothing.

"How did my father come here?"

"In my station wagon."

"I see."

This whole scene is so bizarre that I don't know how to respond. There's no one to ask what to do. My brothers just stand there. Hugo is as inscrutable as a stone carving. I reach into my pocket.

"How much?"

"Seven hundred and fifty dollars, American."

I pull out the wet bills and count out eight hundred dollars. He hands me fifty back in change. He smiles. Everybody's relieved. He shakes all our hands. He tells me it's sad, what happened, and how hard it is for all of us when these things befall us.

The funeral director steps up. He's unctuous, in a suit and hair oil and cologne. His workers are short Indian men in tan work clothes. It's like an optical illusion: the police toady steps away and three reflections of him appear in his absence.

I still have the change in my hand. He starts in—*tragic losses, at rest now, gone to glory, deepest sympathies*—but there is the small matter of the funeral costs.

"How much?" I say.

"Five hundred and fifty dollars," he says. "Unfortunately."

I hand him my change.

"We'll come up with the rest," one of my brothers says.

"We'll take up a collection," says another.

On our way back downstairs, Hugo says, "So much for your present."

I am so confused, I want to cry. I cannot. For years afterward, I will try to cry and be unable to. On some nights, I will take spit on the tips of my fingers and draw tears down my cheeks, trying to find relief.

———

We Mexicans wake the dead. We *give wakes* to the dead. Hugo and I agree that my shift will be at around two in the morning. He leads me to my father's room and goes off to bed. My aunt still shares a room with her mother. I can hear the women in there, snoring. The sounds of Tijuana carry up the hills, somehow different from the sounds of the United States. The dogs, the car horns, the traffic rumble, the whistles, the trumpets are all in a different language. Their pitch and timbre are as distinctive as is Chinese, or Russian. Or Spanish.

I sit in my father's room, listening. All that noise, and the whole world dead. His pillow is still streaked with his hair pomade—he wore it trim, short, combed straight back off his forehead, always as slick as Jerry Lewis'. I can't sleep in his bed. Everything smells like him. I am naked. I am unbelievably aroused. All I can think about is sex. I keep hoping the family's cleaning woman will wake up and come to my room. I want to eat, make love, climb a mountain, have a fistfight. I talk to Jesus. I sit in the middle of the floor and sift through layers of paper: report cards, citations, letters from women in Sinaloa, divorce papers, poems, tax forms, INS papers, bowling certificates, sheets with numbers on them, military records, a letter from the president of Mexico. Silverfish and roaches come forth from my father's pages, where they have lived safely, eating his past.

I pull the string attached to the bare bulb above my head. The dark claps shut around me. Years later, it seems, Hugo speaks from the greater darkness of the doorway.

"It's time."

I get dressed.

We go to his truck.

Everything's quiet. You can even hear crickets. He starts up, puts it in gear. We drive down the dark hill. Everybody's lights are out as we descend.

"God damn it," Hugo finally says. "It's not fair."

He drops me off at the door.

"See you in the afternoon," he says.

"All right."

"Somebody will be by in a few hours," he says.

"All right."

He drives away. I step inside. It's bright, pleasant. Old carpets have loops tugged loose. Inexplicably, there is an electric clock with a soft-drink logo on it. Chapel A has a forgotten casket in it. My father waits in Chapel B.

It's a dull little room with dull little drapes at the end. There are about eight rows of pews. A plywood lectern stands before the raised coffin. And there are all those flowers. Their colors are basically white and carmine beneath the fluorescent lights; the greens look like rubber.

I try sitting in a pew, looking at the coffin. It looks like a gigantic throat lozenge. I prowl the building. Periodically, the Indian men come downstairs. They apparently sleep up there, because their hair is in disarray and their eyes are red and puffy. "Do you want some coffee?" they ask.

"No thank you."

"Coke? Water?"

"No, I'm fine."

They nod, go back up. Occasionally, one will pat my elbow.

I lift the curtains from the wall and look behind them. There is a door near the head of the coffin. I open it. I step into a small parking area behind the funeral home. A dark station wagon is crunching in on the gravel, backing up to a wooden chute that runs down at an angle from the second floor. One of the workers steps out. He and the driver exchange murmurs. They open the back and pull a figure out by its feet. A motor begins to whirr. They wrestle the drooping corpse in its shroud into the chute. Apparently, there is a conveyer belt inside. The body rises and seems to float, going up to the sky, feet-first.

I step back inside and close the door.

I lift the lid on my father. I can count the tiny white whiskers growing in the blackness of his chin and throat. Stains smaller than dimes dot the front of his shirt—stains he would have never allowed in life. One of my sisters wants him dressed in a jacket. A funeral-parlor worker tells me they'll have to go at my father's arms with a mallet to get them loose enough to put the coat on him. Nobody else knows. He wants to make sure I understand. I do. "What does it matter now?" is what I say.

I go to my pew again.

I wait.

A woman who is notorious as a "bad girl" in our family comes in silently. It is nearly four A.M. She is with a florid American. Her hair is as huge as Tina Turner's, her eyes surrounded by hedges of lashes. She seems startled to see me, caught.

"Come in," I say.

"I'm sorry," she says.

It turns out she didn't want to make any scandal, just to pay her respects privately.

The American hangs around at the back of the room. When I nod at him, he says, " 'Zit goin'?"

Inanely, I say, "Pretty good."

She sits with me. She says, "He was always kind to me."

"He loved you," I say.

I am in love with her. I look at the tiniest of wrinkles beside her mouth, I smell her musky perfume and look at her danger- ous nails and tight skirt, and I think I will marry her on the spot. She is the only person in the world who is alive with me at that moment. I smell her, sit close to her. We hold hands.

"I'm not what they think," she says.

She kisses me. Gets up to leave. Says, "Can I see him?"

I let her go up there alone. She opens the box, looks down at him. The muscles in her legs clench tight as fists. She speaks softly. She lowers the lid. When she comes back, she is crying.

"Good-bye," she says.

I nod. The American says, "Take it easy." They walk out the door. I can smell her all over the room.

My father was a big stud. Though he was five seven, you thought he was six feet tall. My mother chased him out of the house when I was about twelve. He was probably the first Mexi- can to ever rub shoulders with the neighbors on our suburban San Diego street. They weren't that crazy about it. Neither was he.

One day, the lady from across the street came over and told my mother that he was seeing a string of women while she was at work. The neighbor wanted to know if they were prostitutes, or what. That was it for my mother. He left in disgrace, and they never spoke to each other again. When he came by the house to see me, she hid in her room, wanting him to think she was gone.

Every Friday night, we went to the Tu-Vu drive-in to watch movies and eat hot dogs.

All these memories come at me, and I wait. I try to sleep—on the pew, on the floor. I can't. I wait all morning. Finally, around two or three in the afternoon, people start to show up at the funeral home. I've been waiting with my father for twelve hours. I'm eager to get it over with.

People shuffle in, avert their eyes. Half-hearted embraces happen all over the room, everybody avoiding the embarrassment of the coffin. My sisters go up and look. A Mexican Pentecostal evangelist takes the podium and begins to harangue us. It's a pattern I have begun to notice at funerals lately: the preacher takes countless cheap shots at the crowd, which is presumably softened up by the recent death and is busy hoping it won't be next. I feel disinterested. Lack of sleep and hunger has made the insides of my ears feel swollen.

We drag my father off to a dismal little hillside cemetery. He takes his last car ride nestled in pointless plushness; satin pillows cradle him inside the darkness of the box. The hearse is muted and stately. We are led by my uncle, Carlos Urrea, heroic motorcycle cop in the stunning Tijuana uniform. Cars stop and wait for us to drive by. Inside, people are watching the procession, saying *There goes the dead guy* through the glass.

On the hill, his box descends. I back away, then turn around. I watch clouds, heavy as trucks, driving across Tijuana.

When the death certificate comes, it says my father died of a stroke. The insurance company will not pay us a cent, since auto coverage is for car wrecks. They insist on proof.

Hugo goes back to San Luis Río Colorado. He enters the police compound and finds my father's car. It's beat to hell—the tires are twisted, the roof collapsed. He shoots a roll of film, then comes home unscathed.

"Somebody killed Papa," he says. "I know it."

I look at the pictures.

"One side of the car's all bashed in," he says. "There's black and white paint on the door."

"So?"

"Cops. They chased him and ran him off the road. Where would he get black and white paint on a red car that crashed out in the desert?"

I don't know—it sounds far-fetched, then it doesn't. Mexican relatives tell me I'm crazy. They tell me to deal with reality. My uncle tells me the authorities wouldn't behave in such a manner.

Since we buried my father, his mother has died. Hugo called me one morning and said, "You know Grandma? She's dead."

My own mother is trapped in a financial catastrophe that continues to deepen. Within three years of my father's death, she is living in a house without heat, without plumbing in the kitchen, with broken plumbing in the bathroom, and without a stove or oven. She cooks on a hot plate.

Months later, Hugo shuffles through his pictures. The car looks red as blood. It looks, at turns, vast and minuscule. I stare at the crooked seats and see my own ghosts and memories, my own hundreds of miles sitting *right there.*

I can't get my eyes off the roof of the car. It's bent down. All the windows are broken. Hugo is right. There's black and white paint smashed into the passenger door. Or are they simply scrapes?

We send the photographs to the insurance company, and we contact the American consulate for help in investigating the accident. The insurer returns the photos and refuses to pay us a settlement, suggesting the pictures could have been taken after my father died from his stroke. Besides, they tell us, there's no proof that it's even his car.

We are again denied the settlement.

The consul contacts me a few days later. After a full investigation into the death of my father, the facts seem to indicate that there can be no investigation of the death of my father. In the months subsequent to his death, the entire police force of San Luis Río Colorado has apparently retired. No officer can be found who was on active duty at the time of the accident, and since the ones who were on duty have retired and left San Luis to enjoy their leisure time, there is no one to talk to. The case is closed. Official cause of death: stroke.

In a final act of desperation, I write to the chief of police of the town. Hugo, when he hears about it, says, "Hey. You'd better not go to San Luis. Ever." He laughs.

An answer comes: the chief calls me on the phone. Or he claims to be the police chief. I realize now, he could have been anyone. In response to my inquiry, he says, he has only one thing to say. And I should remember this thing, I should take it to heart. "It is over, Sr. Urrea," he tells me. "It is better for all of us that you forget it and move on with your life. It is better for all of us," he says, "if there was no accident. Am I clear? There was no accident."

"Yes, sir," I say. "You are extremely, perfectly, clear."

"Good," he says. Then "Good" again.

He hangs up the phone so quietly, there isn't even a click.

Within a month of my final conversation with the police, I receive an envelope in the mail. It is from the head office of the chief of municipal police of San Luis Río Colorado, Sonora. The information is printed on the envelope with various official swirls of ink and a seal of some sort. I expect it's a letter, but it's not.

I find instead a bill on flimsy paper. The bill is requesting the immediate payment of twelve hundred dollars in American currency. This sum will cover, in full, the damages my father caused to city property on the date of January 10, 1977. There is no mention of how these damages came about. When people ask me, I make a joke out of it. I tell them, *I don't know— maybe he fell out of bed really hard.* Nobody laughs but me.

CHRISTMAS STORY

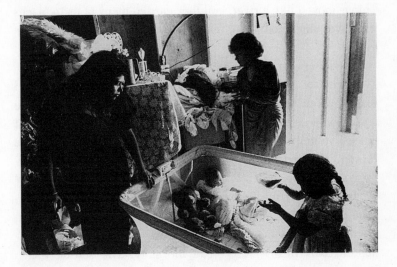

Years later, I returned to duty. I thought I had escaped Tijuana for good, but I should have known. Tijuana is the place from which you never get away.

I'd been away. I escaped the Borderlands in 1982, called to teach in the Expository Writing program at Harvard. There, I met and married my wife. Back in San Diego, however, my mother died. We were left with a decision about what to do with the home I'd grown up in. Ultimately, I couldn't bear to see it sold, so we packed up and moved west in the summer of 1990.

Still, I was not going back to Tijuana. I gave Von a wide

berth, leaving him messages on his office door but not daring to show my face. Things worked out well that way: the poor stayed in Tijuana, and I stayed in San Diego. But then Christmas came, full of strange and wonderful events. I was lucky enough to watch the unlikely series of occurrences take place, to see San Diego and Tijuana join hands for the slightest instant. Things moved like a river, and they carried many of us to places we never imagined we'd reach. This is a chronicle of those events.

When we arrived in California, we were out of money. I had written a few things, hoping to earn some. Among them were several pieces about the border. Fortunately for us, the first place I submitted them was San Diego's alternative weekly, the *Reader*. I thought nobody would care. The *Reader* had a surprise in store for me.

It published the first piece near Thanksgiving, as a front-page exposé. A woman named Cynthia Jeffery, who worked in the advertising and promotion department of an FM radio station in San Diego—91X—read the story. The station was a former border-blaster that actually broadcast out of Tijuana (its call letters were XETRA). Its studios and offices, however, were in San Diego.

Cynthia was moved by the story and wanted to do something for the people of Tijuana. Obviously, the Christmas season was coming. She called me in late November, and she dropped a bombshell: the management at 91X had agreed to make the garbage-dump and *barrio* people the focus of a Christmas project to be called "The 91 X-Mas." Various clubs and bars around town would begin the season by sponsoring "X Nights"—gift-collecting events, complete with toy depositories. Meanwhile, requests for food, clothes, and gifts would go out on the air beginning in early December. Finally, December 21 would be dedicated to a live daylong broadcast from the parking lot of the station; disc jockeys would then accompany us into Tijuana to distribute the gifts. Cynthia wanted to know if I could help.

"What do you need?" I said.

"A minister or priest or missionaries who can distribute the stuff."

"No problem."

"Can you select a neighborhood for us to go to?"

"Yes."

"Can you come for the broadcast?"

I thought she was kidding.

She had no way of knowing that the recession, and "Operation Desert Shield" (it was not yet a "Storm"), had hurt Von and Spectrum Ministries. They were down almost twenty thousand dollars, and when Cynthia called, they had not yet received a single toy donation for their yearly Christmas drive. In many *barrios* and orphanages in Tijuana, Von provided the only Christmas the children ever got. Certain neighborhoods had received every toy for a score of years from Von. Before Cynthia's call, it had looked as though Christmas wasn't going to happen that year.

The selection of a neighborhood was an interesting challenge. It meant I'd have to go back. The *Reader* published an article about my beloved little girl Negra, who had spent her girlhood in the dump and then vanished. I could have written a hundred more stories about the border without setting foot across the line. But the memory of Negra receiving her first doll nagged at me. There were thousands of small Negras all over Tijuana. Cynthia was going to try to touch them all.

The Tijuana *colonia* that had once established itself at Tijuana's garbage dump had changed since the days I'd written about. For example, it wasn't there anymore. The landowner envisioned making a new fortune by clearing out the garbage and building *maquiladoras* (border factories, American assembly plants administered by Mexicans and employing Mexican labor at ridiculously low daily wages). Clearly, he could make more money with industrial plants than by renting the space to the city and buying recycled glass, tin, wire, and aluminum from the *basureros* (trash-pickers), even though he resold the junk at a high profit. The only problem was the *basureros* didn't want to go, and in defiance of him, formed a neighborhood collective that parceled out the land in lots.

The old dump site was now two warring *colonias*, Panamericano and Trincherazo. The active dump had moved several hills farther west. The old central dump area and the pig village had filled with tar-paper huts, then a few wooden houses, and now some stucco beauties were appearing. Rough streets meandered between the houses, and each home had a fence, many still fashioned from the coils of burned mattresses. From what I'd been told, it looked for all the world like a little community.

Though a touch more civilized, life was still not easy on that hill. There was no "officially" running water. (They provided their own by running hoses from a huge water tank on a hill above the *colonia;* a series of rubber tentacles snaked all over the neighborhood, bringing in pirated water.) Electric power had only recently been provided by the city. Power was still often generated by stolen or scavenged car batteries. The only heat came from dangerous fires inside the houses, or even more dangerous braziers of coals, or still more dangerous kerosene burners. If the people weren't overcome by carbon monoxide fumes, they stood a good chance of being burned to death. With the dump closed down, there was no ready work, and few of the families could afford transportation to the new dump, six or seven miles away. Many of those who went there to work got up at four and made small lunches of flour tortillas, then walked.

Some families had discovered that the hillsides in Trincherazo and Panamericano, formed by tractors piling mud and slag over mounds of garbage, could be mined for glass. Incredibly, there were now small trash-mines dotting the slopes, where families pried apart the hard gray-black soil to recover bottles. A fifty-pound gunnysack of glass from the hill brought them $1.50.

Because the *barrios* were built on roughly improvised land-fill, all manner of dreadful substances roiled to the surface. The dust there was not normal dust—it was equal part ash, chemicals, and decomposed biological matter. When it rained, the dirt didn't quite form mud. It formed a kind of noxious pudding that flooded the outhouses and lifted their contents to float into the streets, adding to the miasma. After rain, methane gas seeped out of the soil. The smell of sewage and explosive sub-terranean processes leaked from the ground as though the entire *barrio* were a drowsing volcano waiting to blow.

Though the old dump had changed drastically, and though Negra had been missing from it for years, I still felt connected to the place. I still carried pictures of them all with me, showing them around my various English and writing classes. For all I knew, Negra was dead. On the other hand, she could have simply moved to a neighboring *barrio* and I'd never know where she was. She could have gone home to Michoacán; she could have crossed the wire; she could have died on I-5 running across at San Ysidro, or in Oceanside. There was absolutely no way to know.

In her world, most people don't read or write. There are no telephones, so nobody calls. And if there should be a writer in the bunch, there would be no way to get a letter to anybody, because they live in places with no addresses. There is no place to write *to*. About the best you can do with Panamericano, for example, is to write to the corner store and hope they'll give the letter to the right person. Finally, most of the people can't muster the money to buy postage, paper, or envelopes, should they have an address to which they could send letters. You could move two miles away and vanish forever. Their view of San Diego and the coastline, though, remains spectacular.

There were several other *colonias* around the city that were likely targets for the "X-Mas" drive. In spite of the smell and the dirt, the lice and the dogs stiff with mange, and the violence, Tijuana was a place I loved and had been away from for too long. Writing for the paper had reminded me. And the irony of the situation hadn't been lost on me: once, a few years ago, I had fed these families. Now I was back, and they were feeding mine.

The next time I called Cynthia, we were on: the disc jockeys were already talking about it on the air. I was to take them into a preselected location in the 91X van: both she and their midafternoon personality, Oz (whose on-air promos solemnly pronounced him "probably the worst deejay in the world"), would accompany me across the border and hand out gifts. I didn't want either the radio people or the folks from the *colonia* to get in trouble. Anything was possible—from outright banditry to police raids. If we heaped gifts on one group of people to the exclusion of another, there could be retaliations. (One fellow, who turned out to be Negra's uncle, lived near the new dump. He was rumored to be hoarding money in his shack. He'd been seen that day selling his possessions. He was, in fact, getting ready to return to Michoacán, and had sold his furniture to pay for the trip. It was a less developed area in those days, and his shack was set apart from the others. A gang of toughs, after failing to bust in on him, decided to set the shack on fire and burn him out. The fire killed him.)

In many Latin American countries, too much attention can get you killed. It is illustrative to note that in El Salvador, almost every Salvadoran professional wrestler wears a mask. The saddest thing about it is that safety is entirely up to the momentary whim of those who have the power, which is usually a chopped-down carbine.

We would select a safe *colonia* and arrive on a commando raid: in and out.

Things had changed with Von, too. When I left, the Mexico Crew was still a loose assortment of renegades working out of a Baptist church. It was a motley crew in those days, but eight years had passed, and now the Crew was a Corporation—Spectrum Ministries, Inc. Every single member from my old days was gone. Many, like me, were married and trying to get on with their lives. Some were burned out. Some were so angry at their experience that they cursed Von and all he stood for. A few had become missionaries on their own. Von, whom some of us called "God's Machine," was still there. He was into his sixties and outrunning men and women half his age.

One of his old-timers now ran the drug-treatment center in the neighborhood where the Satánicos lived. We were looking into the area as a potential beneficiary of the gift drive. He invited me to walk with him down the hill, to look at their small compound. We strolled away from the ball court, through a grating wooden gate that opened onto a small yard. There, a family was gathered around a trash fire. He introduced me to them. We shook hands, joked, and they laughed and wished us *"Dios les bendiga"* (God bless you) as we moved through.

"91X!" he yelled. "No way!"

He couldn't stop laughing.

"Praise God!" he hollered.

It was totally dark. He chugged along at a steady thirty miles an hour, and I was trying to keep from tripping over all the rocks.

"This is the clinic we run," he said as we made our way along a cement-block building. "They came and took all our medicine away."

"Who?"

"They. The city. Said we weren't using it right."

Almost nothing was visible on the street. The moon wasn't up. The houses had saffron wedges of candlelight in their windows. Transistor radios were blaring *cumbia* music. Voices could be heard within, murmuring, or laughing, or cursing.

We were at the church. "Right here," he said, pointing to a spot on the dirt at the entrance to his driveway. "They shot a guy right here. He died right here. He was standing around and a car pulled up and they shot him. He was gasping and gurgling. Right on this spot here."

One of the addicts was guarding the driveway.

"*¿Qué onda?*" the missionary said. (What's up?)

"*Nada,*" the guy replied.

"We built this place out of plywood and scrap." He unlocked the door to the little church. Every door in the compound was padlocked shut. The church had a dirt floor, wooden benches. "The cathedral. Not too fancy." Next door, there was a workshed. "Look at this," he said. "The guys build stuff in here. It's part of their rehab. Check out this cabinet."

It was quite nice. They had fashioned it out of sheets of plywood, two-by-fours, hinges. All of it was lovingly sanded and shellacked.

"Pretty nice, huh?"

"What are these?"

Shiny wooden objects were stacked on the workbenches. They seemed to be wooden squares that looked a little like big floor tiles, hinged, with a handle sticking up from the top.

"Tortilla-makers."

"You're kidding."

"No, really. Tortilla-makers. See? You open it up like this, put the dough in here like this, then press down the handle like this. Makes instant tortillas!"

The handmade tortilla press was the main industry of the rehab center. The men got up at five or five-thirty, attended a six A.M. Bible study, then ate breakfast. ("It weeds out the ones who aren't really serious about getting off drugs," the missionary said. "Kind of like boot camp.") After breakfast, it was off to the woodshed to build these ingenious little machines. The profits from the tortilla-makers, selling for ten dollars, helped keep the center running. I bought one.

He showed me the dorm room, a cluttered bedroom of stacked bunk beds, separated by a blanket from a small kitchen area. His own quarters were no better—he unlocked yet another door and led me up a steep homemade stairway. At the top, in a kind of small plywood attic, was his room. Battery-powered lamps illuminated a rough table and bookshelves made from wooden boxes. On the walls hung mounted blowguns and Indian artifacts from his many trips into the South American jungle. His hammock was strung in a corner, its bottom brushing the top of a kerosene heater.

This compound and the youth center nearby would be the focus of one of the Christmas runs, those kids in the street the recipients.

"This is it," he said.

He walked me back out to the street. We talked there for a few moments about private matters of heart and faith. A strange sound at the back of the compound sent him and the one addict on a quick perimeter march, flashlights nervously probing all the darker corners. When he came back, he said, "Cat." We stood around for another minute, then, to my dismay, he said, "Well, good night!" and went back to his room. I looked up the street. I thought, *Oh great.*

It had gotten late. As I walked in the direction of the youth center, I occasionally tripped over big rocks jutting out of the dirt. Ahead, vague in the dark, I could see a group of the Satánicos. Their cigarette ends flared intense red, and seemed to float disembodied like fireflies. I clutched my tortilla press, figuring I could at least break somebody's nose before they got to me. About a hundred yards farther up the hill, a car in the middle of the street turned on its headlights and sat there. The Satánicos were a blue-gray shadow against the light. They were watching me. But, after all, this was Christmas. It was a time for wonders, and as I came even with them, they all called "Good night," and "See you later," and "How's it going?"

I replied, *"Hasta luego,"* and *"Buenas noches,"* and kept walking, touched and relieved.

Back at the youth center, one of the addicts saw my tortilla press. "Hey!" he said. "I made that!" He was beaming as he shook my hand.

But this is not the story I have come to tell you.

Nor is the story of 91X's big broadcast, nor even what came after. Christmas 1990 began once all these events were finished. But we had to go through them to get there.

I pulled into the 91X parking lot at seven forty-five. It was Friday, December 21—a blustery day with early-morning clouds sailing in from the sea. Victor Harris, one of the ace drivers on the old Mexico Crew, slid the Spectrum Ministries van into an executive slot near a small pile of toys and clothes. The radio station staff had already been out there since six. Dwight Arnold, who was officially in charge of the project, was up on a ladder, hanging the black-and-yellow 91X banner over the entryway to the station. Several puffy-eyed suits from the "Mighty 690" AM side of the station stood around gawking, blowing on Styrofoam coffee cups.

A tent stood dead-center, where bagels and coffee were being doled out. Cream cheese in white plastic buckets attracted one homeless guy who was wearing several pairs of glasses at once. He had white cheese hanging in small icicles from his whiskers. I was impressed at how hard he tried to look like a station employee. Later in the day, he caught a chance to slip into the studios through an open door and not reappear.

Bryan Jones, the morning disc jockey, was well into his radio show, and "cutting edge" music echoed off the Highway Patrol building across Pacific Highway. "We're broadcasting live from the parking lot," Jones cried into the mike, "collecting toys for the needy and homeless, and we're *freezing* our *butts off!*"

Later, he would say, "Donate to the homely and needless."

By nine, two large piles of goods had accumulated. David Thomson, guitarist for the mighty Los Angeles rock band Tokyo Burlesque, drove all the way to San Diego to help load toys. It struck me as incongruous that this rocker in his very bad '67 Mustang fastback the color of blood had chugged down I-5 to stand around in the rain putting several hundred pounds of stuff in the vans of a bunch of Baptist missionaries, most of whom wouldn't be caught dead listening to Tokyo Burlesque or 91X.

Cynthia came out to say hello. She was a beautiful woman with a blond mane. "You did this," I said as the steady flow of rock 'n' roll philanthropists dropped off trash bags full of clothes. Somebody brought a clear plastic Winnie-the-Pooh full of Cracker Jacks.

"This is great," Cynthia said. "But wait till Oz gets here."

It was now midmorning. Steve West, an Englishman, took over the mike. He put me on the air a couple of times, but he seemed to think my name was "Ruiz."

Suddenly, the drummer for the Beat Farmers, Country Dick

Montana, made an appearance. He staggered out of the parking lot, saying, "Anybody seen Oz? Where's Oz?"

West motioned the Reverend Dick (mail-order) over to the mike. Already famed for his cheerful dissipation, Dick didn't disappoint, quipping on air that he'd recently barfed. He also suggested people bring in provocative underpants. Then he lurched back into the parking lot and vanished.

The first vanload of toys pulled out, to much hoopla. Another would go out during West's show. It rained. The Trash Can Sinatras pulled up in a record-company van. They had come to play on-air, to help the "lads and lassies" of Tijuana—though I'd lay odds they had no idea who or what that might be. They shuffled around in the parking lot. Gorgeous and indecipherable Scottish-sounding accents ensued. "Hootmon," they said. "Oots a roody hoot tee plee heer!"

They went inside and performed an acoustic set on the air. Then they came back out. Kids had flocked to the parking lot with video cameras and Instamatics, and the Trash Cans (or are they the Sinatras?) gave autographs. After they left, two Asian girls ran up to West begging to see the band. Told the band had left, one of them cried into the mike, "I just got screwed!"

West, unflappable, said, "Right here in the lot?"

Wait till Oz gets here.

They were right: as soon as Oz took over the show, what had already been a successful morning kicked into some bizarre overdrive. Victor took off once, twice, three times with vanloads. Skateboards, surfboards, food, clothes came in. A trucker tore in from the freeway in his eighteen wheeler and handed Oz a ten-dollar bill. Four, five, six vanloads.

Seven. It was coming far faster than we could load it. Even when the Marines hauled away a large pile for the Toys for Tots program, we were having trouble keeping up. By five o'clock, Victor was speeding in and out, hauling the donations up to Pastor Von's offices, and the stuff was apparently rising to the ceiling. After the ninth load, more drivers had to come in—we were running double loads in tandem.

It continued after dark: a ten-speed bike; $140 in groceries, neatly boxed. An unemployed woman pulled up in her car. "I got a blanket," she said. "I was just cleaning a lady's house in trade for a cake. You wanna see the cake?"

We walked to her car. The cake was in the front seat.

She handed me the old blanket. "Wish I could give you more," she said.

Pastor Von finally appeared to be interviewed. On the air, Von told Oz about a group of orphanage kids in Tijuana who had decided to give Christmas to children in the garbage dump. Each child took one of his or her own toys, wrapped it nicely, then went to the dump and selected a child to give it to. I always imagine a hush all over San Diego at that moment, like the hush that befell us all in the parking lot, everybody pausing for just an instant to consider it.

As the last vanloads pulled out, and the torrent of donations finally began to slow, I went inside and collapsed on the couch in the lobby. A "jock" named Pam Wolf was doing the last show out in the dark, wrapped in a blanket. It was raining. A biker rolled up, reached under his leather jacket, and pulled out a teddy bear.

We'd spent thirteen hours out there, and none of us had

really seen what the magnitude of San Diego's generosity was. We had seen it being whisked off, but it would be an hour or so until we got to see how huge it had turned out to be. I had been trying to think of an appropriate thank you for Oz and Cynthia, and all I could think of was to give them my only picture of Negra. They'd huddled shoulder-to-shoulder in the cold wind, the picture flapping between them.

And still, people came. They rattled the door. Cynthia would jump up to open it, and someone would hand her a toy. The last, sweetest thing was what finally overwhelmed her. A young businessman in a shirt and tie appeared at the door with six large coffees. "You've been out in the cold all day," he said. "Take these, and Merry Christmas." She sat on the arm of the couch and cried.

Still, Christmas had not yet come.

Cynthia, Oz, and a group of workers stood in the Spectrum Ministries building and gawked. There was stuff everywhere: toys, clothes, coats, blankets, shoes, cookies, cans of food, bread, candy, bicycles, Walkmen. Some of us sorted out four hundred of the best toys for the next day's "X-Mas." We had selected Trincherazo—the old "Lower Dump"—because it was isolated enough to be controlled. Von was going in the next day to bathe the kids, and they would announce the toys late in the day, before too many hundreds of invaders could hit the hill. Probably, our only invaders would come down from Panamericana. The radio crew and I would swoop in at the last minute.

Late in the night, when all the physical labor was done, we lounged around trying to get to know each other. Efren, one of Von's full-timers, appeared, and he told us a suitably appalling story about one of the dump-people. A man named Jessie had somehow gotten his throat cut and not died. Efren and a young woman were there when Jessie pulled open the rag he'd been using as a bandage. The flap under his chin fell open, and maggots tumbled out of his throat.

The girl vanished behind one of the vans; Efren hurried off to vomit.

Oz said, "I'm going to go vomit right now!" and shut himself in a bathroom.

"But I looked back," the missionary said, "and this girl was cleaning the worms out of the hole in his throat. I couldn't believe it. I said, 'I thought you were vomiting.' She said, 'No. I went behind the van to pray. I asked God to let me see Jesus in that man, and that's what I did. I made believe I was cleaning the wounds of Jesus.' "

That one pretty much capped off the evening.

Victor and Oz made a plan to rendezvous in Tijuana somewhere. I was too tired to pay much attention. We said our goodnights, and we drove away.

The next day, we gathered again in the 91X parking lot, empty now and unexceptional. It was Saturday, December 22, near two in the afternoon. Oz, in the studio, was wrapping up his show. We had Victor's van loaded with over four hundred toys in bags, boxes, and bundles from Von's office. A Volvo pulled up. Three little girls peered out at me; their dad got out and said, "You still taking stuff to Mexico?"

Oz, "Probably the worst deejay in the world," rushed out late. Dwight Arnold was at the wheel of the "X-Van," with Cynthia riding shotgun. We agreed to follow them through the border, since the guards would probably not choose to harass a radio-station vehicle. We sailed through, on our way to our rendezvous with Victor—we thought.

We cut through town, looped up onto the east–west highway that runs to Playas de Tijuana, and we got lost. We looked everywhere for the overpass where Victor would meet us. It was nowhere in sight. We drove through the crumbling dirt canyons that all seem to be crowded at one end with new shacks. At an impromptu recon stop, I hopped in the "X-Van" and we roared off. Suddenly, we were entering Playas de Tijuana and I said, "We missed it. We overshot it." Dwight pulled into a shopping center, and Oz and I began a short series of interviews of Tijuana Law Enforcement Officials. *"Perdone, oficial,"* we'd croon, *"sabe usted donde se puede encontrar la colonia llamada El Trincherazo?"* (Greatly respectful, we spoke in the florid *usted* form: "Excuseth thou us, Officer, but wouldst thou know where we might find the neighborhood called El Trincherazo?")

The cops would all rise up about an extra foot in height, look off, then say, "No."

We were already about a half hour late. I would find out that Von and the missionaries, faced with several hundred cold, restless, and vaguely irked people, resorted to silly busy-ness to avert a minor riot. They lined everybody up in straight lines of fifteen each, and when they had everybody neatly lined up, they moved the lines up and down the hill. After forty-five minutes, Victor gave up on us and radioed that he was coming in. Von, finished with the bathing of the kids, with the giving out of food, with every task available to stall, then resorted to giving out the tickets that would get the kids into the gift room.

Meanwhile, Oz and I were schlepping through the mud of a

depot for water trucks. These rattletrap flatbed trucks—many of them dating from the late fifties—roam Tijuana with huge water tanks in the back, pumping water into cisterns all over town. We figured if anyone knew how to find a lost *barrio*, one of these drivers would. But the one we asked squinted an eye and stared at us. "Trincherazo?" he said, as though tasting it.

"Yeah!" I said. "It was the dump, a couple of years ago. Now it's two *barrios*—one at the top of the hill, one at the bottom. This is the one at the bottom. Near the new factories."

"The new factories! You're on the wrong road for the new factories."

"We are?" Oz and I fairly sang.

"It's the next road. Toward Ensenada. There's an overpass."

"The overpass!"

Back in the van.

"Don't worry about a thing," I lied. "I know *exactly* where we are."

We stumbled on down the road, peering up various arroyos that failed to be our turnoff. Suddenly, there was an off-ramp that said ENSENADA, and it wasn't a lie anymore. The hills connected with my memory—there was the place where water gushes out of the cliff in storms, there was the little whitewashed bridge, and over there was the army base. On its slopes, white stones etched out the insignia of various army outfits—the Fifth Infantry Battalion had crossed carbines forming an ominous X.

"Make a U-turn," I told Dwight.

"Are you sure?"

"Yes, absolutely. Turn around. That's the road up to the old dump."

We turned around and went up the ramp to the overpass.

"Turn right. Up the hill. Trust me."

I hadn't even seen this road for over five years, but it was like my own driveway. "Keep going," I said. Oz and I were crouched behind the seats, kneeboarding the ruts. I told Cynthia, "You're going to see the places you were reading about."

A deadly-looking pair of cops hanging at a house with a bunch of dopers waved us on up the hill—"Just follow the road up and over. It's open all the way down. Just keep going."

"Thank you!" I called.

One of the dopers came at us, shouting, "No Christmas? *'Onde 'stá mi* Christmas!"

"What's he want?" Cynthia said.

"Presents," said Oz. "He's asking where his presents are."

Dwight hit it.

It was stunning, coming over that hill. The dump had been replaced, just as I'd heard. Little houses and shacks and hovels and sheds absolutely crammed every foot. I said, "There, on the right! That was Pacha's house." Cynthia craned. "Over here used to be the pig village!" It was now a row of some of the better houses. "Negra used to live right there!" I tapped Cynthia on the shoulder. "See down there? That's where Jesusita lived."

"The one who got murdered?"

"Murdered?" said Oz. "How'd she get murdered?"

"Somebody blew her head off," Cynthia reported mildly.

"Head?" said Oz. "Off?"

"Turn left!" I said.

They looked out the windows at the ruin. We could have been driving through a movie set.

The dirt track bent down sharply, and we began to pick up followers as we descended. Everyone with a radio listened to 91X down there—many kids in Tijuana consider it the hippest product Tijuana has ever offered the world. There is great loyalty to any call letters starting with "X." *"La radio!"* kids chanted in ones and twos.

Suddenly, a dementedly cheerful black-and-white dog— part pit bull and part who knew what—took the lead. She placed herself directly in front of the van, trotting so close that there were times when her tail brushed the front bumper, and she barked madly at everyone in our path. She looked back at us regularly, with a dog grin on her face, and shouted, "Woo! Woo!" Our canine herald cleared the road, all the way down, and as we made our way through the last lake of cocoa-brown water blocking the road, the crowds came into view. She barked us into the middle of them, then sat down and began to scratch at a flea under her front leg.

I'd opened the van's sliding door on the way down. I crouched in the opening, calling to all the families who had lost heart waiting for us. "Go back! Christmas!"

Oz was shouting, "Go back down! To Von!"

People were waving, calling at us. One really wild little boy trotted beside the van, face nearly black, yelling at me, *"¡Raite! ¡Raite!"* (Ride! Ride!) I nabbed him and pulled him into the van. He and Oz started jiving right away. Then we were nearly there, and a group of women saw me and shouted, *"¡Luis! ¡Luis!"*

I said, "Somebody remembers me after all these years."

We stopped, and I jumped out of the van. The gathered lines of people were freezing and restless. Worried missionaries hustled all over the place with no apparent goal in mind. The

children, clutching their tickets, yelled, "*¡Jugetes!*" (Toys!) and
"*¡Creesmas!*"

Three little girls charged into me, yelling, "*¡Luisluisluis!*"
and kissing me. I didn't know who they were. I looked up. And
Christmas came.

Negra's mother, Doña María, was walking down the hill.
And with her, a pretty young woman, very pregnant, and the
young woman put out her fingers and touched me lightly and
stared at me. She had the smallest hint of blue eyeliner under
her eyes. I looked at María. "Yes," she said. "It's her."

"I never forgot you, Luis," she said. "Did you ever forget
me?"

Negra.

The temperature had dropped to the upper thirties on that
hill, due to the fierce wind. She wore a light sweater, jeans, and
shoes. Her hands felt like something pulled out of the refrigerator. We held each other, wandered around the area. Two of the
little girls were hers—Elsa and Nayeli (a Mixtec word meaning
"Flower of the Fields"). The other girl, Marta, was Negra's
niece. She was the same age as Negra when we first met. Negra
and her mother were raising her.

The next baby was due at any time. I put my hands over
Negra's distended belly. María said, "Get her out of here, Luis.
Get her out."

I wrapped Negra in a blanket. She tucked my hands under
her arms to keep my fingers warm. We looked out at the perfect
view of San Diego; it looked like bronze, the color of wheat
fields in spring.

————

Almost five hundred toys were distributed that day. Every child who came left with a toy. Oz found the dopers and homeboys irresistible—he bravely joined sulking groups of them, handing out key chains and buttons, chatting happily in *cholo* Spanish. Cynthia dove straight in, disappearing into the small building where the gifts were.

Here's how it worked. The toys were laid out in the same building where the baths had been given. They remained unwrapped so the kids could see what they were, and the offerings ranged from stuffed animals and dolls to soldiers, wristwatches, board games, and sports equipment; there were cars, trucks, Barbies, rubber wrestlers, squirt-gun sets, radios, coloring books. These were all spread out on tables and the floor. Von stationed *gringos* at strategic points around the room to prevent general looting. A squad of other *gringos* guarded the door. Each line of fifteen kids was brought to the room, and they turned over their tickets as they went in. They were free to choose whatever caught their fancy. On the way out, they received a mark on the back of the hand so they couldn't sneak back in for another gift. Around every corner of the small building, you could find kids eagerly licking their hands and rubbing them desperately on their pants.

In the days to come, the missionaries repeated this scene at the active dump, at Panamericano, at the Satánicos' *barrio,* and at other *colonias* and orphanages around the city. Today, if you go into any of the tar-paper houses scattered over the hillsides of these neighborhoods, you are likely to find new dolls still in their boxes, or teddy bears on scavenged beds, going gray with the dust of the canyons.

The two new bikes were raffled. Everyone got a ticket, and the stubs were put in a plastic bag. With the bikes, the missionaries raffled off a bear over three feet tall and a plush orange snake about six feet long.

In the neighborhoods where there was no building to distribute the gifts, the vans were pulled into U-shaped half circles, and the kids entered the gap in groups of two or three. Meanwhile, games of skill dotted the periphery, so they could win further things—candy bars, Cokes, paddleballs. It looked for all the world like the fair had come to town. The mothers could be seen, later, hauling the gifts and the food and the candy up the steep cliffsides, their children yelling and laughing.

The thing that leaps out at you at every site is the absence of men. Time and time again, there are families whose fathers have gone across the wire, not to return. And if you look at the chests of the kids and teenagers, you can see scabies pits, and angry little red welts.

Back at Trincherazo, mothers begged for blankets, but there weren't enough for them. Confronted with a group of about twenty women vying for the one extra blanket I carried, I had to choose one woman. It was a dark luxury, to be carrying the only available blanket on that hill. I picked a teenage mother whose baby was wrapped in part of a bed sheet. Elsewhere, kids and winos were encrusted with 91X buttons. They wanted to shake hands with "El Oss." Smiling, he was slowly sinking in a pool of yammering children. An old woman went up to Cynthia and put her frozen hand on her cheek to say thanks. Cynthia took off her gloves and put them in the woman's hands.

Negra had a long climb ahead of her—night was coming on, and the cold was really clamping down. She lived back up the long hill. Victor and I piled her and her kids and her mother in one of the vans. They made us stop to pick up a woman who had recently undergone abdominal surgery, and who was also struggling up the hill, clutching her stomach. We banged up, then, noisy and laughing, Negra holding my hand in both of hers, the little ones admiring their toys. We were like a family for a minute. Marta tucked her head against me, laying her skinny back across my front.

Negra lived in an abandoned chicken coop. She led me inside. Incredibly, it was almost exactly in the same spot where she had lived years before. So much had happened to her—they had fled Tijuana in despair and gone home to Michoacán. Times were no easier—in fact, harder—for them in the south. "At least," Doña María said, "here you have garbage!"

Upon their return to Tijuana, Doña María fell in with a man who brought violence and abuse into their home. Negra had to flee: in her elegant phrase, "Situations obligated me to leave." She was fourteen. She settled in a canyon *barrio* only six miles from Panamericano, but I'd had no way of knowing where she was. There, she had survived. And now, they were back in this chicken shack.

It was dark. The floor was indistinguishable from the mud that slopped in the yard. Gaps in the slats of the walls wider than a finger let the breeze cut through the room. Three ducks wandered through, commenting on the scene. The apparently ubiquitous pit bull delivered kisses to everyone who came near. Negra's one bed had been scrounged out of the trash. We sat on it together, the little ones happy and shiny-eyed.

Nayeli had scabies marks on her belly. Negra's sister had come back for a short visit from her new life in the U.S.—she'd brought them a small artificial Christmas tree. It stood on some papers beside the scavenged stove, on which two frying pans of cold fried rice gave up their perfume. There was one small gift for each of them under the tree, wrapped in jolly Woolworth paper. Negra's sister had gotten across the wire, and she'd managed to marry. She had things like Christmas trees and a house with a floor, with windows, bathrooms.

Negra sat beside me holding my hand. She was still wrapped in my blanket. I don't think I got scabies, though something crawled up under my shirt and gave me a fierce bite, and the itch soon spread into my armpits and across my ribs.

Negra said nothing much. She wanted a picture of my wife and me together. She told me she was suffering very much. "We're getting her tubes tied after this one," her mother said. "It's killing her." Negra's man, Jaime, didn't come home that night.

Elsa, Negra's littlest girl, stepped to the tree and stared at it, transported. She suddenly pointed at it and cried, as loudly as she could, "We have so many toys!"

During the Christmas season, some fourteen people died of the cold in Tijuana. Eight babies died of exposure on Christmas Eve alone. A man in a Tijuana hotel room died from breathing the fumes of a brazier of coals he had lit for heat. Life continued. A desperate twenty-four-year-old prostitute, faced with a newborn baby she couldn't care for, wrapped it up, put it in a

box, and stuffed the box in a trash can near the Tijuana bus
terminal. Fortunately for the baby, someone heard it crying and
lifted the lid of the can. The woman was condemned to prison
for three years.

Workers in the garbage dump told me of the babies they'd
been finding dead in the trash—deaths not reported by the
newspapers. Recently, they were startled to find a mayonnaise
jar with a human hand sticking out of it. One woman told me it
was clearly intended as a message, but nobody could figure out
what the message was supposed to mean.

Most recently, a street girl with mental problems lay down
on Revolución and gave birth on the sidewalk. One can only
imagine the horrified tourists with their arms full of *serapes*
freezing on the sidewalk, not sure what to do.

A couple of times a week, I was lucky enough to go to my
Negra's shack and sit on the bed with her. She had no chairs. I
took her food and clothes, slipped her small things. She said, "I
dream about how your house must be. It must be big. It has
trees. I think they're fruit trees." The baby was coming any day
now. Negra's navel, stretched wide by the baby, felt like a soft
cup through her sweater. She was terrified that she'd have to
deliver the child in her own bed with no medical help. When I
asked her how much it would cost to go down the hill to the
clinic, she hid her face and started to cry, a desperate silent
moment of pure terror. She said, "Seven hundred thousand pesos," and clutched the blankets. Later, at Tacos El Paisano, the
taco-masters figured it out for me on their adding machine:
approximately $237.28.

She had Elsa, the last baby, at the Red Cross clinic downtown. The medical student attending her attempted to do an
episiotomy, where they slit open the bottom end of the vaginal

opening to facilitate the birth. However, he made a mistake, and Negra was sliced deeply, the cut going through her perineum. She nearly bled to death on the delivery table, the student trying to stanch the flow of blood with his hand as he called desperately for a doctor. They pumped blood from her family members into her to keep her alive.

With help from friends, we managed to come up with the money. She had the baby—a girl named Silvia—in February of 1991. The clinic attempted to make her stay an extra night to rest, but Negra insisted on returning home to take care of Nayeli and Elsa. Victor drove.

I often took Negra food for the week. She liked to cook for us, so Victor and I braved the intestinal danger and sat in her small cooking alcove and ate fried beans, salsa, tortillas, and butchered backyard chickens. We had the good fortune to show up at Nayeli's fifth birthday—they had nothing to give her, so we bought her a fancy cake. The neighborhood children came over for a party.

The mothers of those children pooled what they had together and gave Negra a baby shower. *"Un chowerr,"* they called it. They gave her: one bottle of baby shampoo, one can of baby powder, one baby jumpsuit, one set of booties. She still keeps them in a plastic bag hanging from a nail on the wall.

One of the extra benefits of the "91X X-Mas" drive was a load of garage doors donated to Von by a company called All-Pro, in San Diego. Von was in a bind, though—he didn't have the papers to transport the doors, Aubrey was too busy to use them, and the Baptist church was not amused that Victor and I had somehow constructed two six-foot-tall towers of five-hundred-pound doors in their parking lot.

In early spring, we secured papers and loaded the doors onto a flatbed on loan from a *gringo* who lived in Tijuana, teaching Mexican boys perfect English. At Negra's, four *barrio* men rushed to our assistance, and together we unloaded the doors and stacked them in her yard.

Negra's man, Jaime, then built them a new house on a raised cement foundation, where they live to this day.

Negra asked my wife and me to be the new child's godparents—*compadres,* in Spanish. Quite literally, "co-parents." "This time," she said to me, "you and I can finally be related."

"It's an honor," I said. I put my face to her hair. The top of her head barely cleared my chin.

"Do you think of me as a sister?" she said.

"Yes."

"Your little sister?"

"Yes."

"That's how you love me," she said.

There was nothing else to say. It wasn't really a question.

There is not much you can do, but you do what you can, and you dare to hope after all. Heartbreak and hope—business as usual in Tijuana.

CREDIT: BARBARA URREA DAVIS

The author, with Negra.

Luis Alberto Urrea was born in Tijuana to an American mother and a Mexican father. He graduated from the University of California, San Diego, in 1977. After working as a film extra, he joined a crew of relief workers helping the poor on the Mexican side of the border. In 1982, he went to Massachusetts, where he taught Expository Writing at Harvard. Currently, he lives in Boulder, Colorado.